Be Expert with
MAP & COMPASS

THIRD EDITION

Björn Kjellström

Revised and updated by
Carina Kjellström Elgin

WILEY

John Wiley & Sons, Inc.

For general information on our other products and services or for technical support, please contact our Customer Care Department within the United States at (800) 762-2974, outside the United States at (317) 572-3993 or fax (317) 572-4002.

Wiley also publishes its books in a variety of electronic formats. Some content that appears in print may not be available in electronic books. For more information about Wiley products, visit our web site at www.wiley.com.

ISBN 978-0470-40765-3

Printed in the United States of America

10 9 8 7 6 5 4 3 2

Contents

Preface to the Third Edition

Björn Kjellström at his beloved cabin in Sweden in the 1960s.

This book has been around for longer than I have, and I am "no spring chicken," as they say, having just crossed that notorious half-century mark. First published in 1955, *Be Expert with Map & Compass* has become an institution as a guide for generations of people seeking important basic navigational skills. Over 500,000 copies have been sold in English-language editions, and it has been published in French, Italian, and Chinese.

I am always pleased when I meet people from all walks of life who are familiar with, and indeed fond of, this book. From former Boy Scouts to Marines to avid deer hunters to 4-H leaders to search-and-rescue dog teams, I have been impressed by the number of people who become animated when the book is brought up. For many, it rekindles memories of the great outdoor opportunities it led them to; for others, it seems to remind them of younger, simpler days spent fidgeting with the dials and trying to master the mystery of magnetism.

Many things are different from when my late father, Björn Kjellström, last updated this book in 1994, with the help of one of my dear brothers, Tord. International and national-level orienteering has continued to develop into a highly technical sport, utilizing the most modern techniques and materials. Global Positioning Systems, known as GPS, were certainly not a readily available consumer item just a few years ago. This book, however, is still the ideal for anyone who wants to learn the basics of compass navigation, as it helps you get comfortable with map and compass skills and gets you ready to participate in or organize a local orienteering event.

It was "Green Bar Bill," Bill Hillcourt, a hero in American scouting circles, who initially encouraged my father to write this guide. My father had been a Championship Orienteer, on foot and on skis, in his native Sweden, though his passion was admittedly for nature and the compass, not for trophies and medals. An entrepreneur from the start, he registered the company that was to become known the world over as Silva at the ripe age of nineteen.

A few years later, in 1933, he and his brother, Alvar, joined forces with another young orienteer named Gunnar Tillander. Together they made history by producing and marketing the first protractor-compass, the concept of which still defines the modern orienteering compass today. Silva compasses became the standard, selling over 500,000 a year in the United States alone.

In 1946, my father took his first business trip to the United States, during which he helped Scout leaders organize the first orienteering event in the United States, at Indiana Dunes State Park, near Lake Michigan. He is credited with introducing the sport of orienteering to North America, and even with coining the English word "orienteering."

He moved permanently to Westchester County, New York, in the late 1950s. He had the 4,700-acre Ward Pound Ridge Reservation as his backyard, so to speak, and quickly made it a point to clear and mark cross-country ski and hiking trails. A professional orienteering map followed, and soon training events were a regular occurrence one hour north of New York City. He somehow found time to be vice-president of the International Ski Federation and was actively involved in the Swedish, U.S., and International Orienteering Federations.

When the time came to update the book, I took the project on with trepidation. How could you improve upon what was considered a classic? Even though newer books have appeared on the market, it seems there is none better at providing a simple, step-by-step guide to success. I quickly realized there wasn't much I needed to change, though I had a good time modernizing some of the content and some of the Swinglish (Swedish-English) language.

Going through this book page by page reminded me of many days spent by his side in "the Reservation," training scout leaders and other

Carina Elgin with her father, Björn Kjellström.

willing participants. As I retyped the various "practices" given in the book, I remembered being a young girl and doing them all, under his kind, patient eye. He hiked or skied the trails daily, and often, as a child, I would go along, slowing down his six-foot-three pace notably. Frequently, we would stop at a "coffee place" in the middle of the woods, enjoy some juice and cookies, and marvel at the beauty around us. I thank him for so many things, including that love of nature and a very useful innate sense of direction.

In his eighties, the "gentle giant" with the warm wit was slowed by Parkinson's disease. I know he was frustrated when his long legs stopped being able to handle those daily walks through the woods. One of the last days we spent together was on the deck of our summer cabin in Sweden. It was a beautiful day, the kind Swedes wait all year for, with a bright, warming sun and a fresh, gentle breeze. On days like that, the sun has a special way of warming up the scents over there (maybe it's the lack of humidity?), and I clearly remember the soft wafts of the pines and the delicate vapors of the dry, gray moss clinging to the Baltic rocks. Seagulls cawed overhead, and the line from the flagpole clanged a consistent beat.

We sat there relaxing, the soft sun on our faces, savoring, with every one of our senses, this moment of true pleasure put on by Mother Nature. With his eyes closed, he started talking, calmly wondering which way we should go. Should we try that trail? Or maybe that way, where we just saw that deer? He spoke happily, as if he were exploring some wonderful new orienteering terrain. I don't know whether it was the medicines he was taking, or if the Parkinson's was making him delusional, but I sat quietly and listened to the contentment in his voice.

To this day, it has given me peace that in his last days he could continue enjoying his greatest passion. And, I truly believe, he is orienteering still, somewhere.

Carina Kjellström Elgin
The Plains, Virginia

INTRODUCTION
The Art (and Science) of Orienteering

Primitive maps have guided man since our earliest days on this planet. What led us on trade routes, ensured our return from exploration, and helped locate opposing forces in war eventually evolved into the modern map and compass.

In the 1930s, two Swedish brothers, Björn and Alvar Kjellström, were at the top of the sport of orienteering, which requires accurate and fast use of a map and compass to find various markers, or control points, in the terrain. Together with engineer Gunnar Tillander, they developed the Silva compass, and established the Silva Company in Stockholm, Sweden, to manufacture and market their product. What was so different about the Silva system was the clear base, the built-in protractor, and the liquid-filled compass capsule that offered a

1

faster reading. All modern field compasses are based on these developments, which provide speed and accuracy in the taking of bearings, especially key in the sport of orienteering.

Today, most people have learned to understand a map and the directional arrows of a compass in order to navigate city streets, interstate highways, and subway system maps. Now many depend on Global Positioning Systems (GPS), which may make the use of maps and compasses seem outdated and irrelevant.

However, understanding and being able to use these "traditional" tools is as important as ever. Total dependence on GPS-type navigation tools removes the important fundamental skill of independently being able to position oneself in one's environs. What if you exit a hotel on a trip to New York City and have no clue on how to orient yourself? Even if we all soon carry a personal GPS in our cell phone so we "never get lost," a lack of geographical sense locally and globally would sadly leave you dependent on machine or fellow man as you move about.

It is empowering to know where you are, especially through a constant innate sense of direction. By learning to use a map and compass, navigating skills are ingrained and useful in everyday "personal orientation." You can figure out where that bus stop should be or how to get home after a bike ride.

GPS systems can break down, malfunction, or become lost. They do not perform well in foggy conditions and in places where trees, mountains, canyons, and other obstructions block your line to the orbiting satellites that a GPS needs to accurately pinpoint its position. Many of us have television service that is dependent on a satellite and know how bad weather or technical malfunctions can interrupt your favorite movie. Similarly, your GPS could leave you high and dry . . . or low and wet! There are just too many scenarios where a GPS could fail, especially when you are out in nature.

It is imperative to have a backup system to your GPS if you are out hiking, hunting, or otherwise enjoying the great outdoors. Because of their simple, nonmechanical, nonelectrical construction, compasses seldom break. The red arrow very, very rarely loses its ability to point north, as it depends on nature's magnificent, unbreakable magnetic field. At the very least, learn to follow a compass and you won't be wandering aimlessly around in circles. Walk in a straight line, and you may eventually find a familiar landmark, a road to rescue, or a place to ask for help.

Being able to use a map and compass effectively certainly provides an important safety factor, but it also opens up a huge world of fun and recreation. With a map and compass as steady companions, and the ability to use them properly, the art of orienteering—the skill of finding your way not only along the highways and country roads but also through woods and fields, through mountainous territory and around lakes—becomes a useful skill, an intriguing hobby, and perhaps even a new sport.

The sport of orienteering on the elite, international level continues to evolve as a highly technical challenge, beyond the scope of this book. However, *Be Expert with Map & Compass* will teach you the skills you need for safe outdoor navigation, for fun, for hiking and hunting. And it may pique your interest in getting involved in the sport of orienteering at the local level.

The Map and Compass in Your Everyday Life

We all make use of maps and compass directions in our everyday lives, consciously or unconsciously.

When you sit down to plan out a trip, whether it's on foot or by automobile, train, ship, or air, you get out maps and charts and try to figure out the shortest way to go or the best way to go to see whatever interests you, be it historical sites, shopping malls, or fishing holes. Asking a source like MapQuest is useful for many things, and a car or handheld GPS can tell you a lot, but perusing a good old map is still often best. During the trip, you repeatedly consult the map or GPS to check where you are and where you are going (and perhaps, to answer that age-old question "Are we there yet?").

When someone asks you for directions, or when someone gives them to you, your brain automatically attempts to draw an imaginary map of the location. In your mind you see roads as lines, rivers as bands, buildings as small squares, just as they are represented on a map. Just walking or driving to the grocery store involves a mental image of the routes available, and just like in orienteering, you may refer to obstacles that might hinder you and choose a better way. Best avoid that construction at that corner and take a different path. It may be longer, but given the terrain (construction blocking the road), the alternate route should get you there most efficiently.

Orienteering is becoming more and more popular as a challenging cross-country sport for youth groups, such as Boy Scouts and Girl Scouts.

In family orienteering, children may sometimes like a piggyback ride.

Backpackers use orienteering to find their way through wilderness areas.

The Map and Compass in the Outdoors

Thanks to foresighted ancestors, most places in the world today have and will continue to have protected parklands and wilderness areas. People in North America have huge areas of open land and wilderness, national, state, and county parks where outdoor sports of all kinds can be enjoyed. An ever-increasing number of nature-conscious people look forward to meeting the challenge of traveling in unfamiliar territory, striking out on their own explorations along little-used paths, or making their own way cross-country.

These people have discovered that they can have a good idea of what to expect in any geographical area by studying a well-developed map. To interpret and understand the map in the field, they can use a simple compass. They will be confident to leave numbered roads and well-marked trails, and leave the GPS for the highways they are most suited for.

Experienced outdoor enthusiasts have no fear or uncertainty about traveling through strange territory—their ability to use their map and compass will get them safely there and back again.

Foresters, surveyors, engineers, prospectors, and men and women in the armed services all require thorough training in orienteering with map and compass. Many organizations, such as the Virginia Search and Rescue Organization (www.vsrda.org), have *Be Expert with Map & Compass* on their required reading list, so that members always are able to consult a map and compass in the wilderness. Hikers, hunters, and riders need to pay heed and learn to use that map and compass, so that those wonderful dogs don't need to search for you!

If you hunt or fish, you will have done much traveling to your favorite hunting spot or trout stream by map and compass—or paid a guide who knows how to use them. In territory you know well from having traversed it again and again, the lay of the land and the different directions will have become part of your memory. In new territory, however, you will have to pore over maps and use your compass skills to find the best hunting ground or best-stocked stream.

If you are a backpacker, your map and compass will give you a sense of complete independence and freedom of movement. How wonderful to "go where no man has gone before," or at least to feel that way. Whenever you feel like breaking away from the trail, you can travel cross-country with confidence. You can explore your way to the hidden lake or mountain waterfall, knowing that your map, compass, and know-how will get you back to the trail.

If you are an athlete interested in cross-country running, orienteering will add new spice and new dimensions to your pursuit. In addition to the mental and physical stamina involved in running, orienteering calls for mental exercise in using a map and compass to determine the route most suited to your style. If you are fleet of foot,

Search-and-rescue teams are required to have excellent map and compass skills before attempting to find people lost in the wilderness.

maybe taking the longer but flatter trail around the mountain will get you to the control point the quickest. If you enjoy the challenge of clambering up a steep, unmarked hillside, you might prefer to go the shorter but more difficult route over the mountain. You choose your own route instead of following a designated trail by deciding which shortcuts you can handle.

If you happen to be a leader of Boy Scouts or Explorers or of Girl Scouts or Camp Fire Girls, or you're a camp counselor on a cross-country hike, or maybe a teacher with pupils on a field trip nature study, you will readily recognize the need to know the proper use of a map and compass. Passing this vital skill on to the boys and girls in your charge will help them get along safely and securely in the outdoors—a genuine way to build their self-esteem. Map study and compass use can be a great source of a number of interesting games, projects, and competitions, whether you are indoors or around a campfire.

If you are none of the above, but are simply a vacationer in a state or national park or a Sunday stroller in the woods, you will quickly discover that knowing how to use a map and compass will increase the fun of your outdoor experience more than that annoying voice on the GPS.

Map and Compass for the Family

A relaxed hike in the woods or participation in a local orienteering event is the perfect outdoor activity for the whole family, an enjoyable and healthy leisure-time activity for all ages. Young children quickly take to orienteering, as it is a lot like a special treasure hunt! In fact, one company uses the treasure hunt format to teach orienteering skills (see the Map and Compass Resources, page 231). Learning to read a map is fun and can quickly teach children that symbols can be used as a quick way to convey ideas and represent all sorts of things. Using a map and compass puts your imagination to work with life-long benefits.

Teenagers find the combination of mental and physical challenge used in exploratory hikes using a map and compass and in the sport of orienteering particularly rewarding. It's not just testing and growing physical skills, but deciding which route to take that helps decision-making skills evolve. Parents find relaxation in orienteering, as a mental break from work and household chores. Even the older generation can join in the wholesome fun of getting away from it all, where speed does not outweigh wisdom.

The vast majority of American families enjoys weekend outings and spend summer vacations together. Why not encourage a trip to the woods or parklands, instead of a trip to the shopping mall? Why not encourage physical activity with a hike in the woods, and combine it with the cerebral exercise of finding your way with map and compass? Day trips or longer vacations are all the more exciting when you have been where no path goes . . . where you have discovered natural beauties the average visitor misses by staying on the worn trail.

Family orienteering is not just about taking a hike with a purpose—it is learning about nature and the world around us. It is one of the best ways to teach young and old to appreciate the environment in which they live. Get people to know and to love nature, and they will become determined to help save our natural resources.

Map and Compass Bringing People Together

People unfamiliar with map and compass sports, such as orienteering, believe it to be a solitary endeavor—one man running through the woods in search of red and white control points, with only a map and compass in hand.

Actually, it is fun to learn how to use a map and compass as a group. Even if you explore and test your skills alone (though it's best to begin with a partner), getting back together and discussing your route choices and what you saw often becomes a rowdy social event. You'll meet others with a passion for nature and can join various clubs.

There are orienteering clubs all around the world to join, if you want to. Helping organize training sessions and race meets is a great way to interact with other like-minded people. As strong as individual competition is in the sport of orienteering, team events also attract many people to the sport. Faced with the numerous mental and physical challenges of navigating unfamiliar terrain, teammates and competitors alike form new friendships and strengthen old ones.

Proof of the bonding that orienteering fosters can most easily be seen before and after organized events. The five-day orienteering championship in Sweden (Oringen) annually draws 8,000 participants in 170 different classes. Participants, not spectators! Most camp out near the event site, from families to elite competitors. They live in extremely close proximity for a week or two, sharing food, stories, and friendship. It becomes a festival of nationalities, cultures, and ideas, tied together by a passion for the map and compass.

After an orienteering event at any level, or even a beginner's map and compass course, check out the attitude of the competitors. They may be tired, or perhaps even angry at themselves for picking a slower route, but typically they sit down and compare notes with others. Which way did you go? What was that like? What could I have done better? You may be competing with others, but everyone is there to improve their own skills, and comparing notes makes for new friendships and new knowledge.

Using the Map and Compass in Education

During the Persian Gulf War of 1990–1991, newspaper articles revealed that an overwhelming number of people had little or no knowledge of the geography of that region. This fact was particularly unsettling because it applied not only to adults but to young students in the U.S. school system.

Learning to use a map and compass, to "orienteer," can be a key to resolving this problem. The sport of orienteering at its most basic, introductory level, is a wonderful hands-on tool for teaching map reading skills, map creation, understanding symbols, direction, the magnetic field, the compass, the relationship of geographical features to how they are utilized by mankind, and more. By getting out into nature, students can also learn to appreciate the environment. In Scandinavia, orienteering is taught in schools. Teaching orienteering in the schools is a wonderful way to get students mentally and physically involved in many disciplines, including geography, environmental studies, mathematics, and history, in a very direct way. Consider encouraging your local school system or your child's teacher to incorporate orienteering into the curriculum or as an after-school program. They'll either say "Yes," or "Get lost!"

The "Romance" of Orienteering

Learning how to use a map and compass can indeed provide all sorts of enjoyment of nature, of your friends and family, of the competitive spirit. Mastery of the art of outdoor navigation also provides a real sense of satisfaction and self-esteem. There has always been a romantic fascination with people who could find their way through the wilderness and over hidden trails: the Native American, the pioneer scout, explorers, trackers, cowboys on cattle drives. There seems to be an almost mysterious power behind path finding and navigation.

In the old days, path finding was well worth admiration. It was based on a highly developed power of observation and memory—reading the signs of mountain ridges, rivers and vegetation, wind direction and cloud movements, animal tracking, the position of sun, moon, and stars.

Today, of course, it is much simpler. Turn on the Global Positioning System! Obey it, and you should eventually reach your destination. However, gain the knowledge of how to use a good map and a dependable compass, and you will have gained a lifelong skill, and possibly that innate sense of where you are on this planet.

What took old-timers a long time to learn, enthusiasts of today can learn in a matter of hours with this book. When you master the skill, it sticks. You will be able to feel safe on all your outdoor urban, suburban, rural, and wilderness journeys. You will be able to choose the best routes, and alternates when they become necessary. You will be encouraged to explore new places, new campsites, fishing lakes, and hunting grounds. And you may, if you choose, become involved in the exciting sport of orienteering.

Whichever route you choose, you'll be more prepared for the challenges ahead.

PART 1

DISCOVERY
Fun with Maps Alone

There are many ways to imagine looking down upon Earth from above. You've probably peered down through an airplane window and tried to figure out where you were; or you've fooled around on Google Earth (www.googleearth.com) and been fascinated as you've been able to zoom in closer and closer and get more and more detail.

Photos from the Space Shuttle are equally intriguing, as one can see shifting sands and the boot of Italy from so far away. It is also fun to imagine what birds see, especially hawks as they use the currents way up in the sky to glide seemingly effortlessly over our planet.

Imagine you are that hawk, or are in an airplane or even on a magic carpet. It is a bright day, with unlimited visibility. The sky above is blue. Below, the ground spreads out like a multicolored quilt. First, everything is just a jumble, but soon you are able to make out details.

That straight ribbon down there, for example, could be a highway—Route 66, or whatever it happens to be. The wide, winding band must be a river. You can even make out a railroad track, as two parallel lines—the rails. The smaller rectangles are rooftops, the blue spots are clearly swimming pools, and those brown and green diamonds are obviously baseball fields. The dark green masses must be forests. Things look different from what you are accustomed to, and yet you can recognize them.

What Is a Map?

If you took a picture of what you saw on your adventure in the sky, and later printed it out, you would have a photographic "map" of sorts of the area over which you flew. There would be a lot of confusing details that would be hard to interpret, and there would be some distortion near the edges because of perspective. Nevertheless, it would be a map: a reduced representation of a portion of the surface of Earth.

Modern mapmakers use aerial and satellite photographs and then check them using surveying equipment from the ground. In the final version of the map, they simplify details into representative signs they call map *symbols*. They also flatten out the perspective so the map looks the way it would appear looking straight down on it, so that all the distances are in the same proportion on the map as they are in the landscape.

How Were the Earliest Maps Made?

It wasn't very easy for the earliest mapmakers to get a good base for their maps. They couldn't even dream of being up in an airplane to get the bird's-eye view. According to historians in this field, some people today, including the Inuit tribes of the North and indigenous desert tribesmen, show an incredible natural ability to make map sketches showing relative locations and distances between points in an area known to them. Instead of using longitude and latitude lines and compass directions as we do, they usually use a landmark they are familiar with—a road, a shoreline, a ridge, or some other terrain feature—as their orienting baseline for such a map.

The oldest known maps are something like those sketches. The earliest maps were probably first etched in dirt with sticks to show prime hunting grounds. These early maps were very generalized, showing major trails, coastlines, mountain ridges, and possible settlements. The maps would have been greatly affected by the mapmaker's impressions. Ever notice how one member of your family remembers that intersection because that's where the auto parts store is, while another remembers it because of the nail salon?

It wasn't until the discovery of magnetism and the subsequent invention of magnetic compasses that mapmakers could more precisely relate the location of a mapped area to the corresponding land and give precise, scientific information on directions and distances between different points on the map. The first maps or charts produced with the help of magnetic compasses appeared near the end of the thirteenth century, providing a great improvement in accuracy. Improvements in production methods followed with the further technical development of compasses. Mapping methods improved step-by-step until the revolutionary new method based on aerial photography became the standard, now joined by satellite technology.

What Kind of Map to Get

Today there are many kinds of maps to suit a variety of purposes. Almost every person has to make use of city maps, general road maps, or geographic maps. Global Positioning Systems in our cars and cell phones and computer programs such as MapQuest have revolutionized how we find our way around every day, but the ability to read a map will never lose its significance.

Anyone can use a city map or a street map with a little practice. The major streets are named, as are most buildings of interest, such as public offices and churches, or places of special interest to camera-toting tourists. Bus and subway maps are everyday necessities in larger cities.

The majority of road maps are designed to cover a whole state, while others may cover several states or the main cities of a state. In designing state maps, the scale (the proportion of the distance between points on the map and the actual distance between the corresponding points in the field) is decided so that the map will fold (after several attempts) into the familiar rectangles that fill so many automobile glove compartments. A map of New Jersey, for example, may be scaled so that 1 inch on the map equals 5.2 miles of highway. On a New York map, 1 inch may equal 11.2 miles of roads. A Michigan map may have a scale of 1 inch equaling 14 miles, while a map of California may have 1 inch on the map equaling 21 actual miles.

Such maps will help you find your way from town to town, but they will not tell you if you have to travel uphill or downhill. Nor will they provide any information on the topography, the elevations and depressions on the land's surface. Automobile maps are all *planimetric*— from the Latin *planum*, "flat ground," and *metria*, "measurement." Usually these maps do not show elevations, such as hills or mountains. They contain enough detail to help you navigate the highways and roads in your car, but they will not be of enough assistance when you are hiking or involved in the sport of orienteering.

Topographic Maps

The type of map that will best serve you in the great outdoors is called a *topographic* map—from the Greek *topos*, "place," and *graphein*, "to write"—hence, to write or draw a picture of a place or area.

Topographic maps are available for large areas of the United States and Canada. In the United States, they are prepared by the U.S. Geological Survey of the Department of the Interior and are called USGS maps. In Canada, they are prepared by the Surveys and Mapping Branch of the Department of Mines and Technical Survey.

Generally, map symbols on topographical maps (nicknamed "topos") from different countries are similar. If you learn to read U.S. topographical maps, you'll be able to interpret maps from other countries.

Orienteering or Recreation Maps

As the sport of orienteering grew internationally, it became necessary to standardize the maps used for competitions. The representatives from forty-eight member nations belonging to the International Orienteering Foundation (IOF) decided on specific rules and standards for the production of orienteering maps, including colors, symbols, and scales used. They provide much greater detail than regular topographical maps, such as reference to vegetation cover and landforms. They show many small but clearly identifiable terrain features, including small depressions and knolls, streambeds, and distinct vegetation changes, even boulders 6 to 8 feet in diameter.

The development of these internationally standardized maps not only contributed to the growing popularity of the sport among orienteers, but also has increased the interest in map and compass use for hiking, hunting, and backpacking. To indicate their practical use for a variety of purposes, some mapmakers call them recreation maps. Information on areas covered by such detailed orienteering maps can be obtained from the orienteering association of the country you are in. They can also refer you to local orienteering clubs. See the Map and Compass Resources on page 231.

It is no exaggeration to say that it is more fun to travel in unknown terrain with an orienteering map than with a regular topographical map, because it is easier to identify a wide range of features that will help you pinpoint your travels.

What Scale to Pick

Most maps are drawn to a specific scale. A scale is the proportion of the distance between points on the map and the actual distance between the corresponding points in the field. Stated another way, it is the amount that a distance in real life has been reduced for inclusion on the map.

For the sake of simplicity, these map scales have been developed in such a way that it is easy to measure map distances using an ordinary ruler—inches and fractions of inches in the United States; decimeters, centimeters, and meters in countries where the metric system is used. One unit measured on the map represents so many units in the field.

The three most commonly used scales for U.S. topographical maps have been 1 unit to 250,000 units, 1 unit to 62,500 units, and 1 unit to 24,000 units. (Canadian topographic maps are drawn to the scale 1:50,000.) On the map, these proportion scales are indicated by ratios: 1:250,000 and so on. The larger the fraction (1 divided by 24,000 is obviously larger than 1 divided by 250,000), the larger and clearer the details shown on the map. The larger the fraction, the smaller the territory covered by the same-size map sheet, enabling greater detail.

You may be working with an older USGS map, and that is okay, but today you can get USGS maps in the 1:24,000 scale of the forty-eight contiguous states, Hawaii, and the territories. It takes 57,000 maps in that scale to cover that area! Most of Alaska is still covered by the less-detailed 1:63,360 scale.

The scale for an orienteering map has been internationally standardized by the IOF to be 1:15,000. For maps covering small areas and used by schools and for instruction, even larger-scale maps, 1:5,000 and 1:10,000 are being used. They make the maps easier for a beginner to understand, because they are able to show more detail. It is like zooming in and getting a closer look at something.

Why these specific fractions? The reason is simple, and it helps suggest the map scale best suited to your needs.

1:250,000 Maps

The scale of 1 inch to 250,000 inches is almost exactly the scale of 1 inch to 4 miles. The precise figure is 253,440—a number that would require lot of unnecessary work in surveying. Each map covers an area of 6,346 to 8,668 square miles. They were originally done by the U.S. Army Map Service in the 1950s, but are now managed by the U.S. Geological Survey. Later you will be shown how to check the date a map was made, which is important because, clearly, there may have been a lot of changes since the 1950s.

A map on the scale of 1:250,000 will give you a general idea of the geographic features of your region. It will assist you in discovering points of interest within a distance of 100 miles and will prove valuable in planning trips and expeditions.

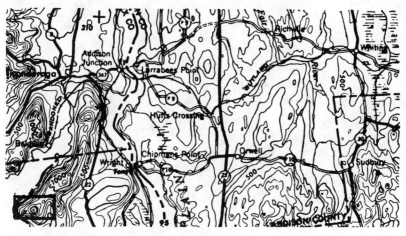

1:250,000 maps will assist you in finding new places to explore. Compare the small rectangle at lower left with the maps on pages 18 and 19.

1:62,500 Maps

The scale of 1 inch to 62,500 inches may seem cumbersome until it is realized that this scale almost exactly equals 1 inch on the map to 1 mile in the field. To be completely correct, the scale should really be 1:63,360, since there are 63,360 inches to the mile, but 62,500 is close enough for most purposes and is simpler for surveying.

Maps on a scale of 1:62,500 are available for most areas of public interest. Each map covers an area that ranges from 195 square miles in the northern United States to 271 square miles in the Southern states. These maps have been replaced by maps in the 1:24,000 scale series for all of the contiguous forty-eight states, Hawaii, and the territories by the USGS.

A map of the area you want to explore on the scale of 1:62,500 or larger would be useful if you intend to cover the area intensively, or to locate suitable terrains for orienteering exercises.

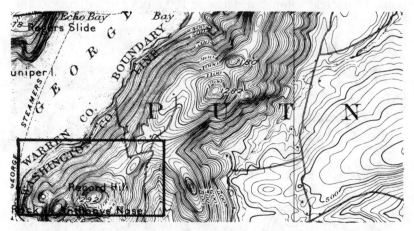

1:62,500 maps are helpful in giving you a general idea of the lay of the land in your area. Compare the rectangle at lower left with the map on page 19.

1:24,000 Maps

Using this scale, a distance of 1 inch on your map is 24,000 inches in the field. That number of inches translates into 1 inch on the map equaling 2,000 feet, a measurement easily used in surveying and in navigating.

Maps on a scale of 1:24,000 are available from the U.S. Geological Survey for every part of the United States, except Alaska. They usually cover areas ranging from 49 square miles (along the Canadian border) to 68 square miles (along the Texas-Mexico border). It takes 57,000 maps in this scale to cover the entire forty-eight contiguous states, Hawaii, and U.S. territories. Alaska is so large that it takes even more!

For finding your way in a limited area within a radius of, say, 4 miles, and for general hiking or orienteering, the map with a scale of 1:24,000 would be your choice (for an example, see page 19).

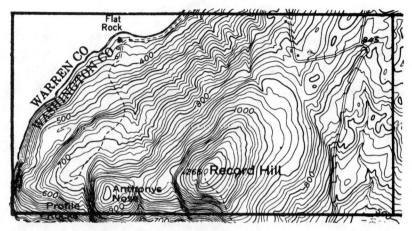

1:24,000 maps are best suited for orienteering because of the great number of details they contain. Compare this map with the maps on pages 17 and 18.

Where to Get Topographic Maps

United States Maps

Many major bookstores and outdoor supply stores sell topographic maps of the local area. You can also get your topographic maps through the U.S. Geological Survey. The USGS and the Internet can also provide you with information on county, state, and national park maps. You can go to www.ask.usgs.gov or to www.usgs.gov/pubprod for a lot of fun information (if you don't have access to a computer, please see the Map and Compass Resources on page 231 for other contact information). You can use the online map locator to find a place of interest to you—say, your home. Instantly, you will be able to choose between a map, satellite, hybrid or topographical map of the area. You can download or order the appropriate map. A downloaded digital map will not provide you with all the detail the USGS topographical map will, so it is best to order the printed map for navigational purposes.

Canadian Maps

For maps of areas in Canada, contact the Canada Map Office at www.maps.nrcan.gc.ca (see resources for other contact information).

Orienteering Maps

More and more areas with public access are being covered by orienteering maps. For up-to-date information, check the orienteering federation for your country for maps and local clubs through the IOF Web site at www.orienteering.org, or the United States Orienteering Federation at www.us.orienteering.org. See the Map and Compass Resources on page 231.

What the Map Tells

We will start our map study on a regular, easy-to-find USGS map. The map is the "reader" for outdoor activities. If you know how, you can read a map as easily as you can read a book. It will tell you what you want to know about the geographical features of an area in which you intend to travel, not just how to get there, as with a Global Positioning System. It does this through the five Ds of map reading.

The Five Ds of Map Reading
1. Description
2. Details
3. Directions
4. Distances
5. Designations

To understand the five Ds, unroll your topographic map, spread it out flat, and take a good look at it.

If you haven't gotten the map you want yet, open up the training map in the back of this book and use that. This map is about one-third of the map surface of an actual USGS topographical quadrangle map on the scale of 1:24,000—part of map number N4345-W7322.5/7.5, to be exact. In printing the map section to fit in this book, we trimmed the margin, but the descriptive matter of the margin was retained; it is inserted in the text that follows in such a way that you will know exactly to which item the text refers.

Description

The description of the map is found in its margin. So let's take a trip the whole way around the margin of a representative topographical map and read all the information pertinent to using the map.

Name of Map Area

The type in the top margin of the map contains the name of the main feature of that map—a town, a lake, a mountain, or some other prominent location or landmark. That is the quadrangle name used in ordering the map.

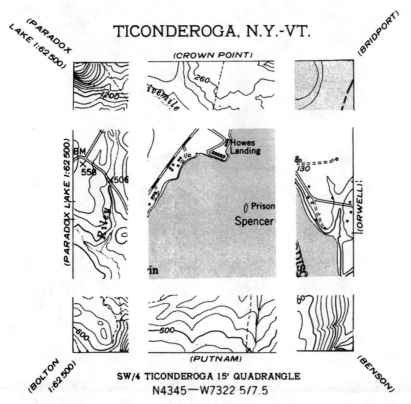

The name of your map is shown in its top and bottom margins. Names in parentheses give you designations of neighboring maps.

This name is repeated at the bottom, with the number of the map.

In small type at the top and bottom, at each side, and at each corner are the names of the quadrangles that border your map. Those are the names you'll use if you want to order maps of the neighboring areas.

Location

Your map is a reduced section of some spot on the planet Earth, but where on the globe? Your map tells you.

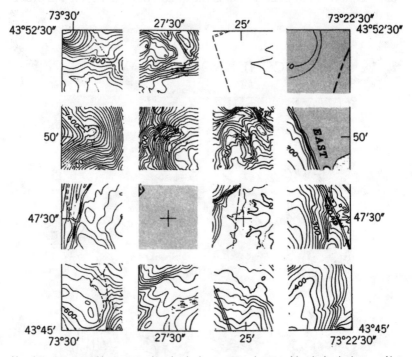

Numbers at top and bottom are longitude degrees; numbers at sides, latitude degrees. Note cross-marks where connecting lines intersect.

At the top and bottom lines that frame the map area, and at each side of the map, are small numerals and tiny lines that jut into the map. With the help of these numbers and lines, you can find the exact place your area is on the globe.

If you connect the tiny lines at the top with the corresponding lines at the bottom, you are drawing *meridian lines* that run true north to true south. If elongated far enough, these lines would eventually hit the North Pole in one direction and the South Pole in the other. The numbers attached to these lines are the degree of *longitude*, figured westward from the zero-degree line that runs through Greenwich, England.

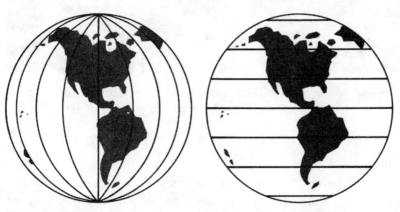

Meridians indicating longitude run from pole to pole; parallels indicating latitude run around the globe. Zero longitude is at Greenwich, England; zero latitude is at the Equator.

If you connect the tiny lines at one side of the map with the corresponding lines on the other side, you are drawing *parallel lines*—lines that run parallel to the Equator. The numbers at these lines are degrees of *latitude*, figured northward from the Equator in the Northern Hemisphere and southward from the Equator in the Southern Hemisphere. The Equator itself has the dubious honor of having the zero-degree designation.

Longitude or latitude—the difference can be remembered by thinking of the origins of the words. Both come from the Latin words used by the Romans to indicate the shape of the Mediterranean Sea. Longitude lines gave the length of the sea, which is longer than it is tall, by measuring from one north-south line to the next north-south line. Another trick is to think of latitude lines as "flat" on top of each other (not next to each other).

Longitude *and* latitude *are from Latin words used to indicate the size of the Mediterranean Sea. Longitude lines give the length of the Mediterranean.*

Dates

At the bottom of the map are some dates of importance to you as a map user. To the left is the information "Aerial photographs taken 1942. Field check 1949–1950." To the right, simply "1950" (see the illustration on page 57).

The map before you was developed from aerial photographs taken in 1942, then drawn and checked by surveyors in the field during the period between 1949 and 1950. The edition you have was printed in 1950. These maps were made by the U.S. Army Map Service, and are now maintained by the USGS. While it was a fantastic and thorough project in its time, you can now get newer, more modern maps of most areas.

A number of things have certainly happened in the area covered since the field check in 1950! If a town is shown, it surely has grown. The road through town may have become a highway. The swamp north of town may have been drained for soccer fields or a shopping center. A dam may have been built across the river to form a lake. Satellite imagery and digital mapping have helped update most areas of the United States. Again, try to find the most recent topographical map you can, through USGS.

A look online at where I live showed that the newest maps were from 1978 and 1984. Of course, there has been development since then. For most wilderness areas where you are striving to use a map and compass, the older topographical maps are fine, because you are exploring natural features, where elevations and rock outcroppings remain the same, rather than recent, man-made ones. So don't worry too much if a few changes have been made since your map was checked. Just take the possibility into consideration when you plan your travels through the area.

Details (Map Symbols)

To show the detail of a landscape, various signs are used called *map symbols*. Map symbols are mapping's alphabet, spelling out the lay of the land in a more efficient way than using letters. These map symbols are not arbitrary code. The people who invented them made every effort to have them look like the things they represent, or stand for.

The main symbols used on topographical maps are pictured in the illustrations printed here. All of them, several pages worth, can be found in the U.S. Geological Survey's free booklet on topographical maps, or online at http://erg.usgs.gov/isb/pubs/booklets/symbols/.

If you get involved in the competitive sport of orienteering, you have to learn to interpret the special, internationally standardized symbols used on such maps. Your local orienteering club or the National Orienteering Federation can supply you with a complete key to these symbols.

To use the USGS topographical maps, you will be primarily interested in four types of map symbols, each with its own distinctive color.

1. Man-made or cultural features: Black
2. Water or hydrographic features: Blue
3. Vegetation features: Green
4. Elevation or hypsographic features: Brown

Man-Made Features

Under the category of features made by people, we have roads and trails, houses and public buildings, railroads and power lines, dams and bridges, and boundaries set between areas. These features are shown on maps in black—with the exception of heavy-duty and

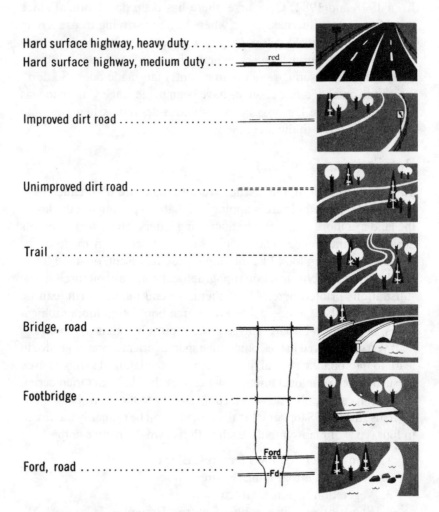

Hard surface highway, heavy duty ....

Hard surface highway, medium duty ..... red

Improved dirt road ....

Unimproved dirt road ....

Trail ....

Bridge, road ....

Footbridge ....

Ford, road ....

Ford
Fd

medium-duty highways, which are sometimes overprinted with red to distinguish them from less significant roads.

Generally, the symbols for man-made features are shown much larger than they should be, for clarity. A road 20 feet wide, for instance, on a 1:24,000 scale map should be only a hundredth of an inch thick, much too thin to be very distinct on the map. Instead, it is shown as

Map Symbols for Man-Made Features—Black

Single track railroad . . . .

Multiple main line track railroad . . . .

Buildings (barn, warehouse, etc.) . . . .

Buildings (dwelling, place of employment) . . . .

School . . . .

Church . . . .

Cemetery . . . .

Telephone, telegraph, pipe line, etc. . . . . .

Power transmission line . . . .

Open pit or quarry . . . .

a double line. If measuring a map involves a road, use the middle of the road as the actual point of measurement. Improved roads are shown as solid double lines; unimproved (dirt or gravel) roads, by dashed double lines. In orienteering lingo, these are often referred to as "tracks." Trails or paths are shown by dashed single lines. Railroads are indicated by full lines with tiny cross-lines to suggest the railroad ties. Isn't this more fun than plugging addresses into a GPS?

Water Features

On topographic maps, rivers and canals, lakes and oceans, swamps and marshes, and any other bodies of water are printed in blue. Brooks and rivers are indicated by a single blue line, larger rivers by a blue band. Large bodies of water are usually shown by a light blue tint, with the shoreline in darker blue.

Map Symbols for Water Features—Blue

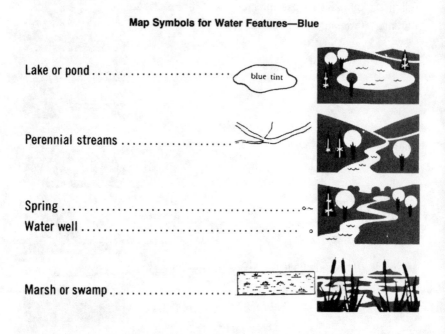

Lake or pond...................... blue tint

Perennial streams ....

Spring ....
Water well ....

Marsh or swamp ....

Vegetation Features

On recent maps by the United States Geological Survey, a green tint is used to indicate wooded areas, orchards, vineyards, and scrub.

For orienteering purposes, it is important for you to know whether an area is wooded or not. Therefore, when ordering your map, specify "woodland copy" to be certain you receive a map with this green overprint.

Elevation Features: Hills and Valleys

The ups and downs of the terrain of an area—its mountains and hills, its valleys and plains—are shown on the topographic map by

Map Symbols for Vegetation Features—Green

Woods — brushwood . . . .   solid green tint

Orchard . . . .

Vineyard . . . .

Scrub . . . .

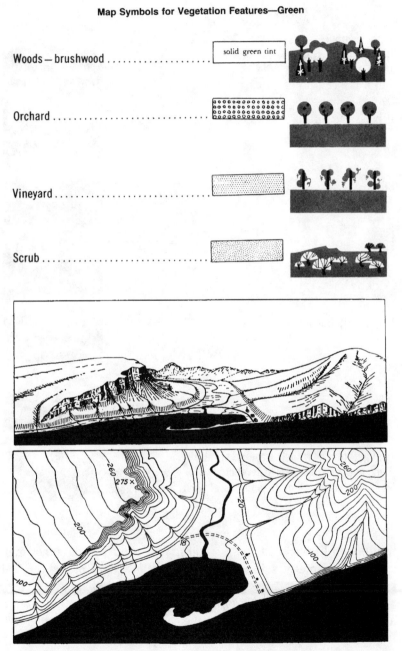

A landscape in perspective above and the same landscape in contour lines below. Note especially that lines are far apart for level land and close together for cliffs.

Map Symbols for Elevation Features—Brown

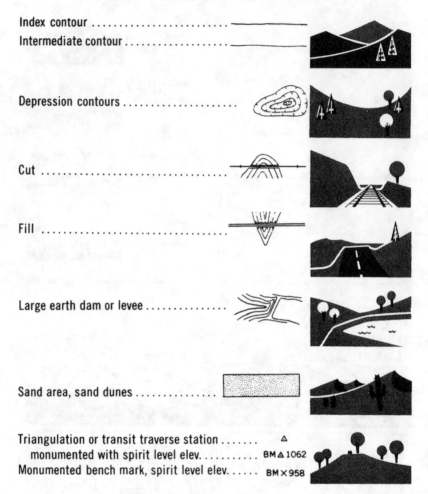

Index contour . . . .

Intermediate contour . . . .

Depression contours . . . .

Cut . . . .

Fill . . . .

Large earth dam or levee . . . .

Sand area, sand dunes . . . .

Triangulation or transit traverse station . . . .   △
   monumented with spirit level elev. . . . .   BM △ 1062
Monumented bench mark, spirit level elev. . . . . .   BM × 958

thin brown lines called *contour lines*. While most of the other map symbols are pretty self-evident, contour lines will probably need some explanation.

A contour line, by definition, is an imaginary line on the ground along which every point is at the same height above sea level (although very occasionally, another reference is used).

Unfold the training map at the back of this book. Study those thin brown contour lines. You will discover that every fifth line—known as the *index contour line*—is heavier than the others, which are called *intermediate contour lines*. Follow one of the heavier lines, and you will find a number on it. This number indicates that every point on that line is that many feet above the average sea level of the nearest ocean, the Atlantic or Pacific. Let's say that the number you have found on the contour is 500. If the Atlantic Ocean should suddenly rise 500 feet above its mean level of zero feet and pour into the landscape, the contour line marked 500 would become the new shoreline.

The distance in height between one contour line and the one next to it is called the *contour interval*. It is the space between contour lines. If the water in our imaginary flood should rise by the number of feet indicated on the map as the contour interval, the next contour line would be the new shoreline.

The contour interval varies from map to map. On a great number of topographic maps—among them the included training map—the contour level is 20 feet. On a map of a rather level area, the contour interval may be as little as 5 feet. On maps of mountainous territories, it might be as much as 50 feet or more. There would not be space for all of those 5- or even 20-foot interval lines. The contour interval of the map you secure from the USGS is found in a note printed in the bottom margin. It may say CONTOUR INTERVAL 20 FEET, for example, but you can figure it out for yourself by studying the numbers on the contour lines of your map.

You'll probably find the contour lines a bit confusing in the beginning, but you will soon look at each hill and mountain in terms of contour lines. When successive contour lines are far apart and evenly spaced, they will indicate to you a gentle slope. When they are close together, they will tell you the area is steep. When they run together, they will show a cliff. When contour lines cross a river or stream, they take on a V shape, with the point of the V pointing uphill. When they denote a spur or ridge of a hill, they become U-shaped, with the bottom of the U pointing downhill. When the contour lines of a hill are far apart at first, then come close together, the hill is a concave hill. It is easy to climb in the beginning, but it becomes more difficult. Where contour lines are close together at

Simple demonstration of contour lines: (1) dip a rock partway in water, draw waterline; (2, 3) dip 1 inch deeper, draw another line; and so on. (4) View from above.

first, then get farther apart, it is called a *convex* hill; hard to climb at first, then getting easier and less steep.

The heights of many points—such as road intersections, summits, lake surfaces, and benchmarks—are also given on the map in figures that show altitude to the nearest foot.

On a map, contour lines show gentle slopes when far apart, steep slopes when close together. They become V-shaped for valleys, U-shaped for spurs.

If each contoured area were cut apart horizontally from the rest, then stacked one on top of the other, the result would look like this.

The whole area would appear as a natural landscape if the map was turned into a relief, as in this training map by the Army Map Service, Corps of Engineers.

Map Symbol Practice

Before you continue, test your knowledge of map symbols. If you are working with others, test them in a way that makes it interesting, using games or practice sessions such as those that follow.

Objective A quick review of map symbols to ensure mastery.

Test Yourself Study the map symbols on page 35. Without referring to the illustrations on the preceding pages, write the name of each symbol on the line below it. Don't peek, now. The correct names are on page 223, at the back of the book.

Just for Fun Copy page 35 onto a blackboard, scan it into your computer, or make as many copies as you have players. Distribute one sheet and a pencil to each player. Give five minutes for filling in the names. Score 5 points for each correct answer, up to 85 points for all seventeen names done correctly.

Map Symbol Relay   **Indoor Practice**

Objective Practice the quick recognition of various map symbols.

Just for Fun Draw the map symbols from page 35 on fifteen 3x5-inch index cards. On the back of the first card, write the name of the symbol from the second card. Thus, the card showing a road would have the word "hill" on the back of it; contour lines would say "cemetery"; cemeteries would say "railroad;" and so on. Make as many sets of cards as you have teams.

Divide the group into relay teams. In front of each team as far away as you choose, spread out a set of map symbol cards, face-up. On the signal "Road—Go!", the first runner of each team runs up to the cards, picks up the card showing the map symbol for road, turns it over, and calls out the written word on the back. In this case, that would be "contour lines." The first player runs back and touches the second runner to let him go. Picking up the contour lines card, the second runner then calls out the word on the back, "cemeteries," runs back to touch off the next player, and so on, until the last card is picked up. The first team to have all cards turned over wins.

MAP SYMBOL QUIZ

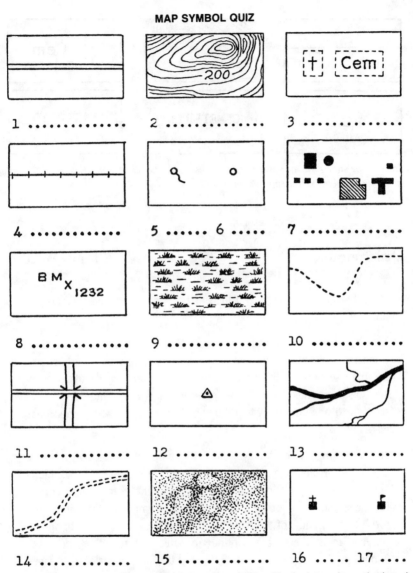

1 ....

2 ....

3 ....

4 ....

5 ...... 6 .....

7 ....

8 ....

9 ....

10 ....

11 ....

12 ....

13 ....

14 ....

15 ....

16 ..... 17 ....

Read instructions for this Map Symbol Quiz on page 34. The objective is to write on the dotted lines the names of the symbols. To use this as a game, have this sheet photocopied.

This game can of course be played outside, too, but it lends itself well to indoor application. You can place the cards far from the players if there is room to run and use some energy, or close by in tight quarters.

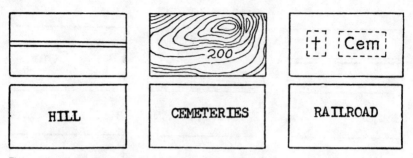

The top line shows the face of the first three cards for the Map Symbol Relay. The bottom line shows the back of the same cards.

Map Sketching

Indoor Practice

Objective To get the general idea of how map symbols relate to one another.

Test Yourself Study a small section of the training map in the back of this book. Get out a paper and pencil. Attempt to sketch, from memory, the map section you have just studied, incorporating into it as many symbols as possible. Particularly important: how roads and rivers run in relation to one another, where buildings are located, where crossroads lead, and so on.

Just for Fun Give each player paper and a pencil, then slowly describe the lay of the land of an imaginary territory. For example, "Draw a highway from the top left corner of the paper to the bottom right corner. Place a spring at the top right corner. Start a stream from this spring, and run it to the middle of the paper until it hits the road. Make a bridge on the road across the stream. Continue the stream on the other side of the bridge, and have it run into a small lake at the bottom left of your paper. Place a school on the right side of the road, just above the bridge . . . ," and so on, using about a dozen map symbols. When the maps are completed, have the players judge one another's maps, and vote to decide which is best.

Objective To be able to read the meaning of contour lines quickly and correctly.

Test Yourself Read the questions, then study the training map and underline the words below that you believe most nearly describe the actual conditions. Answers can be found on pages 223 and 224, but don't look now!

1. You are walking the road from Log Chapel to the crossroads north of it. The road is (a) almost level, (b) uphill, (c) downhill.
2. Charter Brook runs (a) from the bottom of the map to the top of the map, (b) from the top of the map to the bottom of the map.
3. You are walking inland 400 feet on the road from Glenburnie. Your route is (a) a steep climb, rising 100 feet, (b) a slow grade, rising only 40 feet.
4. Sucker Brook is (a) a slow-moving stream, (b) a fast-moving stream.
5. When you stand on the hill marked 400, about one-half mile north of Meadow Knoll Cemetery, you should be able to see (a) Hutton Hill, (b) Meadow Knoll Cemetery, (c) Niger Marsh, (d) Log Chapel, (e) Huckleberry Mountain.

Just for Fun Distribute copies of the training maps to the participants. Then tell them to "find Log Chapel, then follow the road northward to the crossroad. Is the road almost level, or are you going uphill or downhill? How do you know?" The first player to raise a hand and answer the question correctly scores 20 points, and so on, until all five questions have been answered.

Contour Matching

Objective To be able to interpret the outline of hills and to visualize their contour lines; or to determine from contour lines how a hill will look in the landscape.

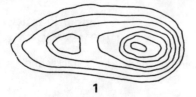

1

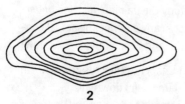

2

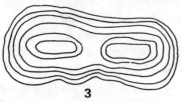

3

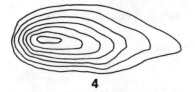

4

5

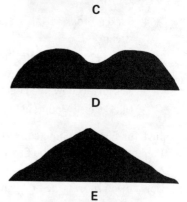

6

A

B

C

D

E

F

The instructions for the Contour Matching Quiz are found on page 39.

Test Yourself Study the hill silhouettes and the contour lines on page 38. Match each hill outline with its correct contour configuration by writing down the letter of the hill next to its contour numeral. Check the result against the answers on page 226.

Just for Fun Three games are possible:

Contour Matching Run off as many copies of page 38 as you have players. Have each player match the hills and their contours, as described in the text above.

Outlines to Contours Use only the copies of the hill outlines. The players are then challenged to draw the contour lines of the hills, as seen from above.

Contours to Outlines Use only the copies of the contour diagrams. Players are to draw the outlines of the respective hills.

....

Directions

A quick glance at a map will show you the relative direction in which any point lies from any other point. But when you want to find the actual direction between two points as related to the north and the south of the landscape, you need to know first of all what is north and what is south on the map as a whole.

Which Map Direction Is North?

When you place a topographical map before you with the reading matter right side up, you can be quite certain that convention has been followed, and that what's up is north and what's down is south. Thus, the left margin as you look at the map is west and the right margin is east. A simple way to remember the order is that it spells "WE" (west on left, east on right).

If there is any doubt in your mind about how the directions lie on your map, look at the bottom margin. Here you will find a small diagram of an angle with one leg marked "True North" and the other leg marked "Magnetic North," but don't bother with that just yet. Simply satisfy yourself that the line marked "True North" runs parallel to the lines that frame the map on the left and on the right.

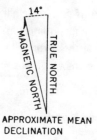

The declination diagram in the bottom margin of the map indicates the angle between the true-north and the magnetic-north direction of the map area.

What Direction Is It?

Now spread your topographic map out in front of you—or use the training map in the back of this book. Find a longitude number along the top line of the map frame and the corresponding number along the bottom line of the frame. With a ruler and pencil, draw a line between the two marks at the longitude numbers. This north-south line is one of the meridian lines described on page 23.

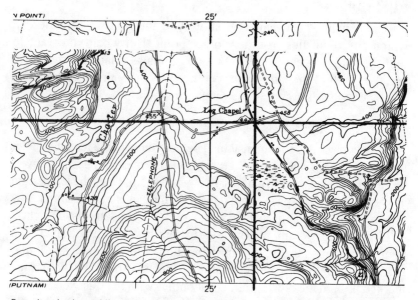

Draw longitude meridian lines, then a parallel through your "base of operations." Find out what lies north and south, east and west, of the base.

Decide on some specific spot on this meridian line, and make that spot your "base of operations" for your practice in determining directions.

First, follow the meridian from your spot up toward the top of the map—any point on the meridian line will be directly north of your base of operations. Follow the meridian line down toward the bottom of the map from your spot, and any point on the meridian line will be south of your spot. Go directly left of your spot, and any point will be west of the spot. Go directly right, and any point will be east of the spot.

Finding Map Directions with a Paper Circle

But what about all the many other directions from your base of operations?

To help you determine some of those directions, take a piece of paper, about 3 inches square. Fold it with sharp folds in half, then in quarters, then in eighths, and finally in sixteenths. Round the free edge with scissors. Open up the paper and mark the folds clockwise: North, North-North-East, North-East, East-North-East, East, East-South-East, South-East, South-South-East, South, South-South-West, South-West, West-South-West, West, West-North-West, North-West, North-North-West, North. To make things simpler, you can just put N, NNE, NE, ENE, E, ESE, SE, SSE, S, SSW, SW, WSW, W, WNW, NW, NNW, N.

Place this circular piece of paper with its center directly over your spot, or base of operations, with the fold marked "North" (or "N") lying north on the meridian line that runs through your spot.

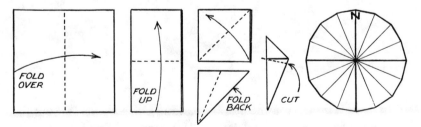

To make a paper-circle protractor, fold a 3-inch square of paper into quarters, then into sixteen segments. Trim to circle shape.

Now, to go in different directions from your base, you may follow the fold marked "NE" and continue into the landscape along this north-east route, or you can go south-south-west, or in any of the sixteen directions you marked on the paper circle.

From Paper Circle to Protractor

The paper circle with its sixteen direction markings is your first step toward using a *protractor*. As you probably know, a protractor is an instrument used for measuring angles. It consists of a circle made from a piece of metal or plastic marked in the 360 degrees of a full circle. The markings start with 0°, go clockwise around, and wind up at the 0° mark with 360°. Zero degrees and 360 degrees coincide. Some protractors, for ease of carrying, are semicircular.

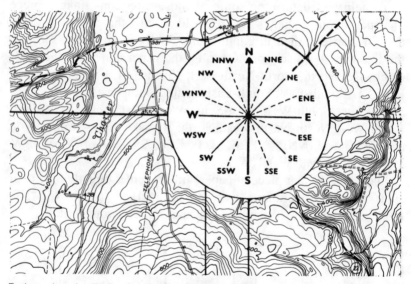

To determine what lies in other directions from your base of operations, make use of a folded paper circle. Place the center of the circle over your base.

In using a protractor, the 0/360° marking indicates north. South is then how many degrees? Did you say 180? Correct! East is 90, west is 270. Northeast is 45, Southeast 135, and so on. With that information you can turn your paper circle into a primitive protractor. Just add the degree numbers at the appropriate direction names.

N: 0 and 360	NNE: 22½	NE: 45	ENE: 67½
E: 90	ESE: 112½	SE: 135	SSE: 157½
S: 180	SSW: 202½	SW: 225	WSW: 247½
W: 270	WNW: 292½	NW: 315	NNW: 337½

It is obvious that for exact degree figuring, your folded-paper protractor will not be very accurate. Your homemade gadget will assist you in learning the principle of the use of a protractor, but if you want to determine correct readings, you need the real thing.

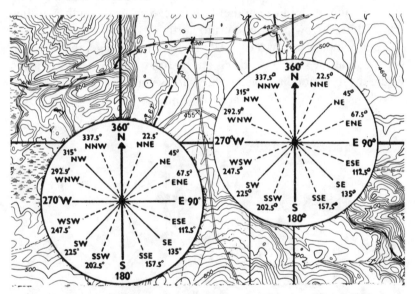

You can turn your folded paper circle into a simple protractor by adding to it the degree numbers of a circle. Zero and 360 degrees coincide.

Finding Map Directions with an Orienteering Compass

In the modern orienteering compass, the circular compass housing is attached to a rectangular transparent base plate in such a way that it can be turned. This adds a protractor-ruler feature to the compass's regular function. The Kjellström brothers and Gunnar Tillander of Sweden, orienteering compass innovators, are the inventors of this feature, and it made their compass brand, Silva, the industry leader.

When you use an orienteering compass for determining map direction, the compass housing with its 360-degree markings becomes your protractor; the base plate with its straight edge, the ruler. The clear base plate allows the map to show through underneath.

Place the compass on the map in such a way that one edge of the base plate touches both your starting point and your destination, with the direction-of-travel arrow on the base plate pointing in the direction of the destination.

Now turn the compass housing with its 360-degree marking until the orienting arrow lies parallel to the nearest north-south meridian line with the arrow pointing toward north.

Your compass is now "set." All you have to do to get the direction is to look at the degree marking on the rim of the compass housing where the direction line touches it. There is your direction in degrees. Easy? It sure is, with an orienteering compass.

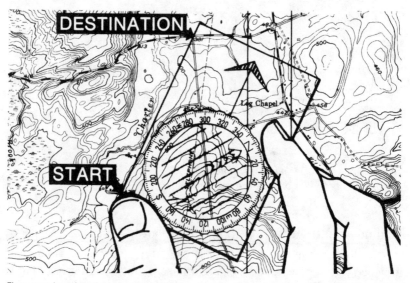

First step *in using the orienteering compass as a protractor: Place base plate on map in such a way that one edge touches both your start and your destination.*

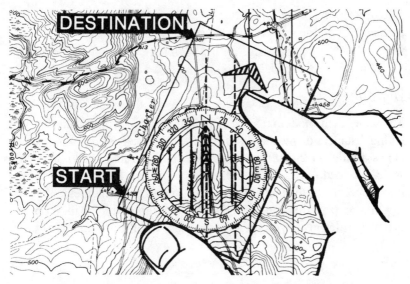

Second step *in using the orienteering compass as a protractor: Turn housing with orienting arrow parallel to meridian. Read degrees over the black index pointer.*

Direction Quiz   Indoor Practice

Objective To practice determining degree directions on an actual map with the protractor-ruler of the orienteering compass.

Test Yourself Open up the training map and use your orienteering compass to find the directions in degrees between the following points:

1. From road-T in Glenburnie to the top of Record Hill _____ °
2. From Record Hill to the crossroad south of BM 474 _____ °
3. From the crossroad south of BM 474 to Camp Adirondack _____ °
4. From Camp Adirondack to Log Chapel _____ °
5. From Log Chapel to Meadow Knoll Cemetery _____ °

(The correct answers are found on page 224.)

Just for Fun Provide each player with a training map and a compass. Read each direction one at a time: "What is the direction in degrees from the road-T in Glenburnie to the top of Record Hill?" As soon as a player has determined the degrees, he or she raises a hand. If correct within

5 degrees, the player scores 20 points; if wrong, the next player has a chance to win, and so on, up to 100 points for all answers correct.

....

Distances

The scales in the bottom margin of your map give you the means for measuring distances on the map. These scales are usually given in four ways: (1) as a ratio—1:24,000 or 1:62,5000; (2) as a ruler, known as a "bar scale," divided into miles and fractions of miles; (3) as a ruler divided into thousands of feet; and (4) as a ruler divided into kilometers.

On a map in the scale of 1:24,000, you know that 1 inch on any ordinary ruler gives you directly the number of miles on the ground.

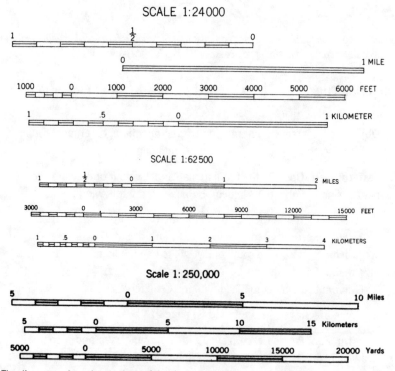

The distance rulers—bar scales—of the three most common map scales as shown in bottom margins of topographic maps. Copy to the edge of a piece of paper for measuring.

Using the Map's Bar Scales

To use the bar scale on the map itself, mark off along the edge of a piece of paper the map distance between two points for which you want to find the actual distance, then measure it against the bar scale in the bottom margin of the map. Or you can copy the bar scale on the map along the edge of a piece of paper, and use this homemade ruler. A rough way of measuring distance is to put your thumb across the bar scale to see how wide it is in miles or kilometers. Then use your thumb to check distances on the map.

Orienteering Compass as Ruler

Even simpler: use the base plate of your orienteering compass for measuring. On some orienteering compasses, the base plate is marked in inches and millimeters or with special scales. Others carry 1:24,000 and 1:62,500 scales for direct reading. There are orienteering compasses that have interchangeable scales that can be slipped over the front edge of the base plate.

Some models of orienteering compasses have distance rulers printed along two edges of the base plate. This simplifies the job of taking map measurements.

You can convert the front edge of the base plate of any orienteering compass you have into a measuring device for the specific map you are using. Simply attach a piece of adhesive tape along the edge and copy onto it the bar scale, in feet, of your map.

Map Measurers

Another method for measuring distances on the map is to use a map measurer. This has a small wheel with which you follow the line between your two points on the map. The wheel is geared to a hand that turns around on a dial on which you can read the distance directly in the circle of figures for your particular map scale.

Distance Measuring

Practice distance measuring until you reach the point where you can look at your map and judge distances on it with fair accuracy.

Distance Quiz   **Indoor Practice**

Objective Practice in measuring distances on the map.

Test Yourself Transfer the bar scale on the training map to the edge of a piece of paper or cardboard strip, or use your compass to find, on the training map, the "as the crow flies," shortest direct distance in feet between the following points:

1. From Log Chapel to Meadow Knoll Cemetery _____ feet
2. From Meadow Knoll Cemetery to top of Hutton Hill _____ feet
3. From top of Hutton Hill to Glenburnie _____ feet
4. From Glenburnie to top of Record Hill _____ feet
5. From top of Record Hill to Log Chapel _____ feet

(Correct answers are on page 224.)

Just for Fun Each player has strip of paper or cardboard, pencil, and training map. The leader asks, "What is the distance from Log Chapel to Meadow Knoll Cemetery?" The first player with the correct answer within 50 feet scores 20 points, with a 100-point maximum for the correct answers to all five questions.

Designations

Place Name Designations

Places and other map features are designed by name in various lettering styles. Regular roman (upright) type is used for places, boundary lines, and area names, while hydrographic names, or water features, are in *italics* (slanting type).

Hypsographic names—elevation features—are given in block letters. Names of public works and special descriptive notes are in leaning block letters.

Place, feature, boundary line, and area names

Richview, Union Sch, MADISON CO, C E D A R

Public works—Descriptive notes

ST LOUIS, ROAD. BELLE STREET, Tunnel - Golf Course, Radio Tower

Control data—Elevation figures—Contour numbers

Florey Knob, BM 1333, VABM 1217–*5806 – 5500*

Hypsographic names

Man Island, Burton Point, HEAD MOUNTAIN

Hydrographic names

Head Harbor, Wood River, NIAGARA RIVER

Place names are printed in varying lettering styles to make it easier to determine what kind of landscape feature is meant.

Designation of Unmarked Locations

There will probably be many occasions when you'll need to indicate to someone else an exact location on the map that is not actually designated with a place name. The simplest way to do this is by making use of the place name that is closest to the location.

Let's take an example: Look at the training map in the back of the book. Find the place name "Huckleberry Mtn" (mountain). Then locate the crossroads 1½ inches south-west of the letter "H" in "Huckleberry Mtn." You could simply write, "Crossroads 1½ SW 'H' in Huckleberry Mtn," underlining the letter you want to indicate. All your companion has to do now is measure from the bottom edge of the letter "H" 1½ inches (taken from the bar scale in the margin of the map, or from a regular ruler, or from the ruler along the side of the orienteering compass), in a southwesterly direction, and there is the crossroads. In other words, he or she finds the place name, then the letter, then the distance and the direction.

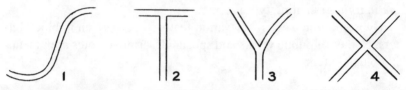

Terms designating road types spell "STYX": (1) Road bend. (2) Road-T. (3) Road-Y or road fork. (4) Crossroads or road-X.

Place Location Practice

In the addition to the examples given below, figure out for yourself how to describe other locations in orienteering language.

Finding Places on the Map  **Indoor Practice**

Objective To familiarize yourself with the method for designating unmarked locations on the map.

Test Yourself Locate the following places on the training map and write down on the line what they are:

1. 2" S "R" in Record Hill _____
2. ¾" E "e" in Charter Brook _____
3. 1 5/8" SE "U" in PUTNAM _____
4. 1 3/16" WNW "H" in Hutton Hill _____
5. 1 1/8" N "l" in Log Chapel _____
6. 5/8" NW "M" in Meadow Knoll Cem _____
7. ¼" N "k" in Sucker Brook _____
8. 1½" NE "l" in Record Hill _____
9. 5/8" W "L" in Log Chapel _____
10. 7/8" S "l" in Huckleberry Mtn _____

(Correct answers can be found on page 224.)

Just for Fun Copy the list above on a blackboard or give each player a copy to fill out. Score 10 points for each map location correctly identified for a total of 100 points for all ten places located.

....

Using a Grid as a Locator

For designating a specific map location, instead of a reference such as so many 1/16ths of an inch north-east of the letter "y" in "Huckleberry," a simple grid system can more simply and accurately accomplish the task. The British Isles, for example, use a national grid system that can pinpoint a location to within 10 square meters.

A grid is a network of intersecting vertical and horizontal black lines superimposed on a topographic or orienteering map. Each of the vertical, or north-south, lines is assigned a specific number in a sequence, as is each horizontal, or east-west, line. These numbers, when quoted in pairs where lines cross (grid coordinates), can designate a specific square on the map.

In specifying a grid coordinate, the north-south line is read first, followed by the east-west line. A grid square is designated by the intersection of the grid lines at the lower left corner.

The area encompassed by a grid square can be determined by the individual orienteer. However, to communicate positions effectively with another orienteer, it's critical that both use the same grid scale. In the British national grid system, for example, each square defines an area of 1,000 square meters. The sides of these squares may be subdivided, using the imagination, into tenths, resulting in accuracy to within 10 square meters.

Experimental Grid System ✴ **Indoor Practice**

Objective Create a grid system on an orienteering or topographic map that will allow designation of specific locations.

Test Yourself Visit a graphic arts supply store and buy a sheet of transparent acetate with a superimposed metric grid (many office supply stores also carry them). Number the vertical lines sequentially from left to right and the horizontal lines from bottom to top.

Overlay the transparent grid onto a contour map and tape it in place. Find specific landmarks and identify the squares in which they appear by reading the grid coordinates. Remember, the vertical line is read first, then the horizontal line.

Practice with friends by giving them specific coordinates and asking them to identify the dominant landmark in that designated area.

....

Traveling by Map

Now that you know the features of a map, it is time to take a map walk. Decide on a place to start your trip, lay out an appropriate route on the map, and try to follow it in the field.

Try an Imaginary Walk First

To give you the feeling of a typical map walk, unfold the training map and take an imaginary walk on it.

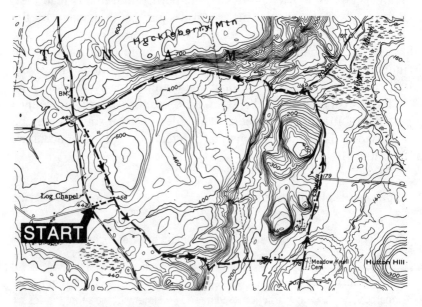

Follow an imaginary map walk (described on pages 52–60) on the training map in the back of this book. Begin at START and proceed in a counterclockwise direction.

Let's say you decide to start from the crossroad south of Log Chapel and take a hike that will bring you in a counterclockwise direction—east, north, west, south—along the route shown on page 51.

You arrive at Log Chapel, then proceed south to the crossroads, and are actually ready to start out. But in what direction? Do you go straight ahead, to the left, to the right, or straight backward?

Orienting the Map

The simplest way to know what direction to go on a map is by orienting the map. To *orient* a map means to turn it in such a way that north on the map fits north in the landscape, and that terrain features shown on the map, such as roads and rivers, are lined up with these features in the field.

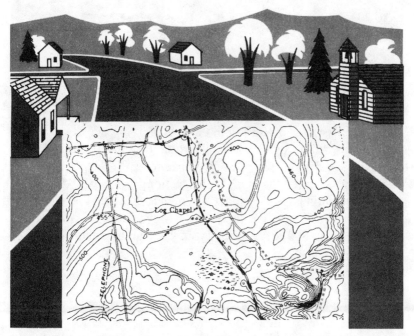

Compare the map with the landscape: Log Chapel is on the wrong side of the road, the road ahead bends in the wrong direction, etc. The map is obviously not oriented.

Compare the map with the landscape: Log Chapel is on the correct side of the road, the road ahead bends in the proper direction, etc. The map fits the landscape, is oriented.

So inspect the map and your surroundings. Twist the map around until the crossroads on it fit with the actual crossroads at which you are standing, with Log Chapel in the right location. The illustrations on page 53 and above provide a good example.

You have oriented the map "by inspection."

The whole thing is simple now. The road to take is to the left of you. And to be extra certain, you have an easy way of checking that it is the right one: about 800 feet ahead of you, you should strike a road-T.

Determining Distances

How do you know when you have walked 800 feet?

The best way of determining distances in the field is *by your step*—or even better, by your *double-step*, or *pace*, counting off each time you put down your left foot—or right, if you prefer.

People have been measuring distances this way since the Roman times.

Have you ever wondered why a mile contains the peculiar figure of 5,280 feet? For the reason that 1,000 double-steps of the average Roman soldier at the time of the Caesars was about 5,280 times the length of the foot of that same soldier. The Latin for 1,000 double-steps or paces, *mille passus*, was later abbreviated into our English "mile."

This will give you a clue as to the length of your own double-step. It will be in the neighborhood of 5 feet—and for general uses that figure is close enough.

If you want to be more exact, measure the length of your double-step once and for all, and remember it. To do this, lay out a step course. Drive a stake in the ground and measure out a distance of 200 feet with a tape measure. Place another stake there. Then walk from stake to stake and back again, counting your double-steps. Be sure to pick a comfortable, determined pace that you can repeat. Divide the complete length covered—400 feet—by the number of double-steps taken. This will give you the length of your average pace. If you covered

To determine the length of your step, lay out a step course 200 feet long. Walk it twice, then divide the number of steps into the 400 feet covered.

it in 80 double-steps, your average double-step is 5 feet. If you used 90 double-steps, each double-step is closer to 4½ feet. (Children love this exercise, and will do it over and over!)

Another way to determine the distance you have covered is *by time elapsed*. This is shown schematically in the drawing below. The times given are for each mile covered—fifteen minutes, for instance, for walking 1 mile along a good road, twenty-five minutes along a trail, and so on.

Number of minutes to cover 1 MILE	HIGHWAY	OPEN FIELD	OPEN WOODS	MOUNTAIN & FOREST
WALK	15	25	30	40
RUN	10	13	16	22

You can estimate the distance you have traveled by the number of minutes elapsed. Various speeds and terrains influence the time needed to cover 1 mile.

The Importance of a Date

You start walking toward the road-T, but before you reach it, you are puzzled by a road leading off to the right. It shouldn't be here. It isn't on the map.

What has happened? Simply this: your map, as indicated on the frame of it, was last revised in 1950—and much can have happened since 1950, and apparently did! What happened in this particular instance was that a building lot was sold, a house was put up, and a road was constructed leading into it from the road on which you are standing.

Topography from aerial photographs by multiplex methods
Aerial photographs taken 1942. Field check 1949-1950

Polyconic projection. 1927 North American datum   EDITION OF
10,000-foot grids based on New York coordinate system,   1950
east zone, and Vermont coordinate system

Dates are important. Your map was correct when last revised—but don't be surprised if changes have occurred, especially if you use an old edition.

You should be able to get a newer map from the U.S. Geological Survey, but maybe you are just using Grandpa's old map to practice with. Remember how all of the United States was mapped by the U.S. Army Map Service around 1950 using aerial photos and follow-up field checks? This is one of those, and you should definitely see if there is a newer map of the area you want to explore before you head out!

Of course, even the newest, most up-to-date maps available are very likely to be missing some things. So be aware of the last revision date of the map, and of the possible changes that can have taken place. A secondary road may have been improved into a primary road. A marsh may have been drained for farmland or may have been turned into a pond. A forest may have been cut down, or a wood lot may have been planted. It can be fun to go to the USGS Web site and see the aerial photos there, which are updated on a five- to seven-year cycle, and to take a look at "your area" on Google Earth. But your map is still your tool for navigation purposes.

After you have set your mind at ease regarding this unmapped road, you proceed—and sure enough, you hit the road-T exactly at 800 feet.

Along the Road

At the road-T you orient your training map again and turn southeastward along the right "arm" of the top line of the T. Second-growth woods are all around you on rather level land—as it should be, according to the map, since the contour lines are far apart. You cross an overgrown brook, and soon after, the improved road turns into an unimproved one. The map is right again—the thin parallel lines that indicate the road type become broken lines.

The road swings to the east and starts dropping toward the south with a steeper drop. You have reached the road-Y, coming in on the left arm. In the crotch of the Y, you change direction and go northeastward

Whenever you reach a prominent landmark or a turn in your route, take time to orient your map. You will then always know exactly where you are.

along the Y's right arm. You are in flat country again, with a meandering brook and a small lake on your right. The unimproved road gets better, and soon you find yourself at the road-T opposite Meadow Knoll Cemetery—a typical country graveyard with a number of old headstones.

You orient your map again, then turn left, northward on the highway. For greater safety, you walk on the left side of the road, facing the oncoming traffic.

According to schedule, you pass an old country church at your left and a side road at your right. Ahead of you, to the left, rises a steep, tree-clad cliff. How steep is it? Plenty steep—just look at those contour lines; they are right on top of each other. How high? Locate the number 179 on the map at the point where the side road strikes the highway—that's the elevation of that particular point. If you choose to go straight up the cliff, you cross the light 180-foot contour line and the heavier 200-foot line, then several light lines, the heavy 300-foot contour, more light lines, and then the heavy 400-foot contour line. The 400-foot line is closed to indicate the top of the hill, but there is another closed line within—the 420-foot contour. It is a very steep and difficult way to go, even in your imagination!

The view from that hill should be pretty good, and you decide you want to get to the top of it. You would not, however, want to climb the cliff wall, so you look at the map and see that the hill slopes up more gently from the north. So you walk up the road a piece—about 2,000 feet beyond the side road—and climb the hill from there, a relatively easy ascent. You were right—the view is spectacular all over the valley, over fertile fields and lush green marshes toward distant hills.

Down and northward again along the road you walk until it swings northeast. There should be an unimproved road to the left. If that's the road, it surely is unimproved. But it must be right—there's a farmhouse and a couple of barns close by in exactly the same relative location to each other as the symbols on the map. You take a chance on the road and soon discover that it is correct enough, because the cliff wall of Huckleberry Mountain rises high on your right as you hike along the lane.

Eventually the road improves, and you can see cars whizzing by on the main road that lies ahead. But just before you reach the main road, you turn left onto an unimproved road to keep away from the main road traffic. Soon you reach a familiar point—the road-T you passed on the trip out. A few more feet along the road to the right—the same 800 feet that formed the first leg of your journey—and you are back at your starting point, the crossroads south of Log Chapel.

Now for an Actual Outdoor Walk by Map

Your training map walk was a fairly simple one—especially since you took it reading these pages and not actually walking! Now it is time to get out your map of your home or practice territory, plan a trip on it, and take an actual walk by map through your own countryside. Don't be too ambitious the first few times. A walk of 4 to 5 miles should give you a good idea of the use of a map.

In the Landmark Hunt project you learn to orient a map and to locate important land-scape features on it. Pointers can be made from scrap wood.

Outdoor Map Practice

As soon as possible, get out in the field and make use of the knowledge you have just gained. *Indoor practice* is useful, but *outdoor practice* is more like the real thing.

Landmark Hunt   **Outdoor Project**

Objective Practice in orienting a map and in locating landmarks.

Group Activity Bring the group to a relatively high point with good visibility, where a number of different landmarks can be seen. Provide each player or buddy team with a topographical map of the area, a pencil, and a list of landmarks to be located on the map as in this example. (Obviously, you must use real landmarks you can actually see from your position!)

1. Draw a circle on the map around the point where you are now standing.
2. Circle the church approximately NW of here.
3. Circle the crossroads approximately S of here.
4. Circle the dam approximately ESE of here.

And so on, for ten landmarks on your landscape.

Set a time limit for finishing this project, such as twenty minutes. Score 10 points for each landmark correctly found and circled on the map, up to 100 points for all ten.

Note: Instead of using a list of landmarks, which at best can only be approximate, and to add more interest, put up a number of markers in a circle about 30 feet in diameter, each marker pointing to a different landmark. You can use strips of wood or poster board, maybe 1 x 2 x 10 inches. One end of each marker is pointed like an arrow, the other end carries a strip of cardboard with a description of a landmark to which the marker points—such as "church," "bridge," and so on. The markers should be at about eye level on wood stakes. Players move clockwise from marker to marker.

In the Map Point Walk follow a route marked by colored streamers. The object is to locate and mark on your map certain landmarks you pass.

Map Point Walk — Outdoor Project

Objective Practice in following a route and locating landmarks found on the way on the map. The Map Point Walk is an especially good preliminary project for promoting a general interest in orienteering. Almost anybody can participate, since little skill is required and because there is no chance of anyone getting lost! Also, any number of people may participate, from a small group to a very large one.

Group Activity On a map, lay out an appropriate route of 2 or 3 miles leading through a number of easily identifiable landmarks. Then go over the route in the field and mark it by tying colored streamers (1-inch-wide strips of red crepe paper or plastic) to trees, posts, or sticks at such distances that the next marker along the route can readily be seen from the preceding one. Hang a wider streamer or regular orienteering marker and place a north-pointing arrow marker at each of the main "landmarks" on the route to assist the participants in their maps.

Send out the participants at two-minute intervals, each provided with a map and a pencil. The object is to follow the marked route and indicate on the map, by circling it, where each of the streamered landmarks is.

The scoring may be done on a time basis, with the person getting the most landmark indications in the shortest amount of time winning. If the landmark indications are incorrect, you can add a five-minute penalty to the participant's time for each error in marking.

Note: In the case of a large group of participants (twenty or more), it will prove advantageous to station a judge at each of the landmarks to score the participants for that specific location. Otherwise it will take a long time at the end to go through and judge all the maps.

Map Point Reporting
Outdoor Project

Objective Combining map reading and observation to provide greater enjoyment of traveling by map.

Group Activity On a map locate six to ten clearly indicated landmarks over a 2- to 4-mile route. Then hike to each landmark and develop a suitable question regarding objects found there or terrain features seen from that spot. For example, what kinds of trees are growing there, what large buildings can be seen, and so on. Decide on an appropriate scoring value for each correct answer, so that the harder ones earn more points. Start

In Map Point Reporting each participant tries to find half a dozen or more landmarks and copies a code letter or performs a project at each landmark.

the participants at two-minute intervals, each with a map, a pencil, and a report card describing the location of the landmark, the task to be accomplished, and the score values for the answers. The object is to score the maximum number of points within a three-hour time limit. The participants decide for themselves in what order to visit the landmarks, and how many they feel they can manage to cover in the given time period. They may decide, for instance, to first locate the landmarks with the highest score value and then try to cover as many of the others as possible within the time limit. Completed report cards are turned in to the judge at the finishing point and scores are computed.

....

PART 2

EXPLORATION
Fun with the Compass

Your upbringing and your formal education play undisputed roles in determining your character and career path. Also important in the "nurture and nature" of who we become are individual experiences, which clearly influence our attitudes and decisions about involvement in a new activity, hobby, or professional endeavor. What if Beethoven had never been introduced to the piano?

Biographers often point to such experiences in the lives of famous people, including one of the greatest geniuses of all time, Nobel Prize winner Albert Einstein. It is said that he did not learn to speak until he was three years old. He hated school and dropped out at the age of fifteen. He failed the entrance examination to the Polytechnic Institute of Zurich. But Einstein referred often to when, at the age of five, his father gave him a magnetic compass. He said when he saw its needle in the grip of the mysterious natural force of magnetism, he was filled with a sense of awe and wonder that never left him.

I suppose that no one will give that compass the entire credit for Einstein's intense lifelong involvement in science, but any youngster's first encounter with a magnetic compass typically results in a similar expression of surprise and fascination.

I clearly remember when my father gave me my first compass. I was so captivated, I did not even want to put it down to eat or sleep! Since then, my compass has led me on many more exhilarating explorations, helping me learn more and more about nature and, in the process, about myself. It has escorted me on uncharted paths in the wilderness, allowing me to feel brisk mountain breezes, smell the rich full scent of the forests, and cool myself in rollicking streams. I've watched wildlife play in habitats untouched by humans, even contemplated on numerous occasions the beauty and agility of a single butterfly flitting from flower to flower in a woodland meadow.

I realize I would not have been able to gain access to such isolated locations were it not for magnetism, the mysterious force of direction. Of all the elemental forces given to us by God, magnetism fascinates me the most.

Just a few intriguing properties:

- A magnet's (lodestone's) field extends beyond its physical measurement. It can penetrate even a solid object, influencing a magnetic item positioned on the other side.
- By mere contact a magnet can impart its strength and polarity to another piece of iron.
- If a magnet is broken into smaller particles, each piece will possess a polarity and attraction identical to that of the whole.
- A magnet has the ability to discriminate between poles. It unites itself with a dissimilar pole of another magnet and repels an identical pole.

But most important to explorers through history, and to you wanting to learn to navigate through nature, magnetism infuses life into a compass needle. The inanimate strip of metal has no visible power source, yet it tirelessly aligns itself with the vast magnetic field of Earth.

There is no doubt in my mind that someone with the intellect of Einstein, eager to find answers to the most difficult questions related to science, would find even a small magnetic compass a source of permanent inspiration. Even if you are not going to become a great scientist, you can make good use of a compass in many situations in life.

You don't need an elaborate and expensive instrument for your first studies. Just get an inexpensive compass. Notice how Earth's magnetic force field influences the needle wherever you move, causing it to point in one specific direction—north—all the time.

—Björn Kjellström

The Origin of the Compass

Details on the discovery of magnetism cannot be found in the pages of history books. Nor can anyone say with certainty who created the first magnetic direction finder, but many historians credit the origin of the compass to ancient China.

A very long time ago—estimates say around A.D. 80—some clever person in what is now China discovered that a piece of a certain ore, floated on water on a piece of wood, would swing until one end pointed in the general direction from which the sun shone halfway between sunrise and sunset. They knew this direction as south, and if one end of the floating ore pointed south, the other end obviously pointed north.

The first real mention of a compass came around A.D. 1050, when Shen Kua, a Chinese mathematician, wrote about the use of a navigational instrument with a magnetized iron needle. Soon afterward, in A.D. 1100, another Chinese, Chu Yu, wrote that sailors traveling between Canton and Sumatra relied on a magnetic-type instrument for navigation.

The history of the compass goes back more than 800 years. Records show that the magnetized compass needle was used by Chinese sailors around the year A.D. 1100, by Arabian merchants around A.D. 1200, and by Scandinavian Vikings in A.D. 1250.

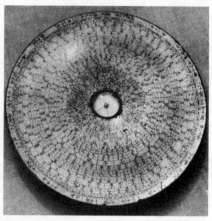

Early Chinese compasses (right) were made of lacquerware, painted with figures and symbols.

Diptych compasses (left) were made in Europe from ivory by such Nuremberg craftsmen as Hans Ducher (1576) and Hans Troschel (1624).

Octagonal silver sundial compass (right) was made in Paris by Claude Langlois around 1725.

Today's orienteering compass (left) has developed from the part-metal prototype of the 1930s into the modern, plastic-type compass that has turned orienteering into a worldwide sport.

Slowly, historical references to the compass grew more common. Arabian merchants and Viking explorers were said to have begun using the device in A.D. 1200 and 1250, respectively.

Development of the Compass

After the invention of the compass needle, someone got the bright idea of protecting it by enclosing it in a metal case. In the beginning, this was a simple air-filled brass housing in which the needle swung around freely, suspended on a point. Such devices are called *air compasses*, or *standard compasses*.

The next step was to find a way of braking the swinging of the magnetic needle so that it would come to rest quickly, instead of having to wait and wait while the needle swayed and jittered. Different methods were tried. In some modern compasses, the magnetized needle swings in a copper-lined housing, and in its swinging sets up electric currents that bring the needle to a fast halt—the so-called *induction-dampened compass*. The most effective method, used in most modern compasses, is to fill the housing with a liquid that slows down the jiggling of the needle and brings it to rest quickly—the *liquid-filled compass*.

Until comparatively recently, the compass housing was marked with the thirty-two points of the mariner's compass. The four main points on a compass are called the cardinal points: north, south, east, and west. The intercardinal points are between the cardinals: north-east, south-east, south-west, and north-west. Then some other imaginative person suggested the 360 degrees of a full circle. Because of this, the compass today shows 360 different directions, or bearings, instead of just the thirty-two of the old-fashioned compass rose.

Finally, the conventional "watchcase" compass was improved into the modern *orienteering compass* in which the compass housing revolves on a transparent base plate that acts as protractor and direction-finder. This type of compass was invented in Sweden in the early 1930s by the orienteering champion Kjellström brothers and engineer Gunnar Tillander. The resulting Silva system took the guesswork out of direction-finding and has become the industry standard, since emulated by other manufacturers. This invention made the use of map and compass easy and accurate.

The Compass Needle Points to Magnetic North

The same force that attracted the primitive compass needles of early explorers—Earth's magnetism—still exerts itself on technologically advanced, modern-day compass needles. Earth is a tremendous magnet, with one end in the north, the other in the south. The north end is the Magnetic North Pole, toward which the north end of the compass needle points when at rest.

If you are one of those people who like things to be uncomplicated, you would want to have the Magnetic North Pole coincide with the true, or geographic, North Pole. Unfortunately, it doesn't. The Magnetic North Pole, which attracts the compass needle, is located about 1,400 miles south of the true North Pole near Bathurst Island off the northern coast of Canada.

Compass Point Practice

In the following pages there will be many references to the sixteen most commonly used, traditional compass directions. Before proceeding, familiarize yourself thoroughly with these compass directions.

The marine compasses of today show not only the traditional compass direction designations, but also the 360 degrees of a circle.

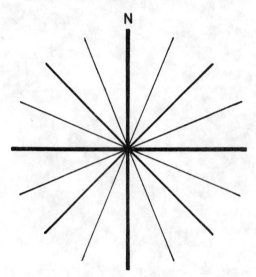

Objective To learn the sixteen traditional compass directions.

N

Study the compass rose on the preceding page, then get out your pencil and write down the names of the sixteen traditional compass points.

Test Yourself Study the compass rose on page 70, then quickly mark the sixteen points on the figure above.

Just for Fun Provide each player with a copy of the figure on page 70. On the signal "Go," each player starts to fill in the names of the sixteen compass directions. The player filling in the figure correctly in the shortest time wins.

Compass Facing **Indoor Practice**

Objective Quick review of the sixteen compass directions.

Test Yourself Stand in the middle of the room facing a wall. Designate the spot on the wall directly in front of you as North. Now quickly turn

Compass Facing is a simple game for practice in memorizing the main compass directions. It can be played indoors as well as outdoors.

your body to face North, then South, West, East, North-West, South-East, North-East, South-West, North-North-East, South-South-East, West-South-West, East-North-East, North-North-West.

Just for Fun Have participants stand up in lines, an arm's length apart in all directions. One wall of the room is designated as north. On the signal "North-east, go!" all turn to face what they believe to be north-east. On the command "Freeze!" stand motionless. Those who are facing the incorrect direction must leave the game. Continue until only one player is left. You can also play by having those who face the directions correctly leave the game to give more practice to those who are still having trouble.

Compass Design Basics

All compasses have one detail in common: the magnetic needle. The needle can vary with respect to the quality of the magnetic steel and the kind of bearing, whether synthetic sapphire bearing or something else. Some needles have luminous points, visible at night, on their north end. Usually the needles are colored blue or red on the north-pointing end, white for the other end. Most needles swing on a sharp-pointed steel pin and are enclosed in a housing, usually round.

Most compasses nowadays, even the less expensive ones, are liquid-filled to dampen the swinging of the needle. Some compasses have housings that are mounted on a rectangular plate of wood, metal, or plastic. Others have housings that are capable of turning on the plates.

To indicate directions, compasses have either a 360-degree scale or a graduation in cardinal or intercardinal points (N, S, E, W, NE, SE, etc.). The graduation may be either fixed in the bottom of the compass housing or printed around the housing's circular rim. Some compasses have special sighting devices, such as prisms, lenses, mirrors, or other constructions.

Some compasses allow you to eliminate the problem of magnetic declination. Others have small lights for night reading. And now you can get compasses with added GPS systems.

You will learn how to use different types of compasses in this book, but it is still vital that you carefully read the instruction booklet that comes with yours.

Examining Different Compass Designs

For many people, the word "compass" elicits the image of a direction finder resembling a watch. Inside, a magnetized needle sits delicately suspended on a point that's centered on a ring marked in 360 degrees or graduations. Early military compasses, cereal box compasses, and pirate movie compasses come to mind.

Even this conventional compass can guide us anywhere we want to go, especially when combined with a topographic map. Having no refinements such as a direction indicator or a sighting device makes these compasses less accurate for cross-country navigation. The modern orienteering compass (see page 68) is more precise for finding routes across unfamiliar terrain, and comes in two basic styles: the thumb compass and the protractor-type compass.

The thumb compass is often used by athletes participating in competitive orienteering. It is a relatively small compass positioned on a clear plastic plate that attaches to the thumb with a fabric strap. A sighting line extends outward from the compass, more or less parallel with the thumb. This type of compass is favored by orienteers who like to have the map constantly oriented and in the same hand as the compass. It allows them to read map details quickly as they pass them in the field, and allows them to adjust direction simply by resetting the sighting line. It also keeps one hand free at all times for balance or swatting away branches. It is generally recommended that you understand the protractor-type compass before trying the tiny thumb compass.

The much more common protractor-type compass is worn around the neck on a cord. It consists of a revolving compass housing on a transparent rectangular plate that's marked with a directional sighting line, orienting lines, and several map conversion scales.

The popularity of the protractor compass is based on its giving directions simply, without requiring the user to go through the intermediate step of mentally checking degree numbers. It provides return direction information without the necessity of adding or subtracting numbers, thus eliminating the possibility of an error in calculations. When used with a map, this instrument combines compass, protractor, and ruler in a single tool.

Traveling by Compass Alone

For safe travel through unknown countryside, it is best to have a map of the area, a GPS if you have one, *and* a compass. In many situations, a map is not available and, as mentioned before, a GPS may fail. There are some hunters and outdoor enthusiasts who think a compass is all that's needed.

Even if you get accustomed to exploring without a map, you should always try to keep a "mental map" with a fixed orienteering line—such as a highway, where you parked your car, or a trail or a creek—indicating the directions between key points. It's great practice to have a mental map with you at all times when driving or walking through a city. Keep the mountains on your left or the Empire State Building to the right. Get used to picturing your position and movement on the planet.

But a mental map has its limitations. What if you forget what you told yourself to remember? If you have no map on hand, you should carry a "find-your-way" notebook and pencil. A notebook can very easily be extended to include your own personal maps of areas you might want to return to. You can include important addresses and phone numbers, directions to your favorite secluded fishing hole, or where you saw the bear and her cubs.

There are three main purposes for which you can use the compass alone—without the help of a map:

1. Finding directions, or bearings, from a location
2. Following a direction, or bearing, from a location
3. Returning to your original location

The Conventional Compass

The conventional compass is the watchcase type—a magnetized needle suspended on a point in a round compass housing marked in 360 degrees. It has no special refinements, such as a directional indicator or a sighting device.

The conventional compass is generally of the watchcase type. The compass is oriented when the north part of the needle lies over the north arrow on the bottom of the case.

Finding Directions with the Conventional Compass

Let us assume that you are standing on an elevated point or open ground and you want to know the directions, or bearings, to various landmarks around you—a distant hilltop, a church spire, a water tower, or a tall tree.

Squarely face the landmark for which you want to determine a bearing and hold your compass steady in front of you with one hand. With the other hand, slowly turn the compass housing until the north part of the compass needle rests over the "North" marking of the compass housing.

Now sight across the center of the compass and read the number of degrees on the compass housing directly opposite your face. This simple procedure reveals the direction toward the landmark, expressed in degrees.

It is obvious that this kind of sighting and reading will give you a figure that may vary a number of degrees in either direction. That is why the better-quality compasses of the watchcase type are provided with a sighting device containing a lens (lensatic compass) or a prism (prismatic compass) through which the reading is done. But those devices increase the cost substantially without materially adding to the usefulness of the compass. A true orienteering compass will help you get the most accurate reading.

Following a Direction with the Conventional Compass

Let's say that you want to explore the distant hilltop you can see from where you are standing. You decide to reach it by traveling cross-country through the landscape that lies before you.

You determine the bearing to your destination by the method described in the preceding paragraphs and find it to be 140°. *Remember that number!* Even better, jot it down, for sooner or later, you will start to wonder whether you remember it correctly or not.

Start walking toward your destination. In the beginning it is easy, because you can still see the hilltop ahead of you. But suddenly it disappears from sight. You have been walking down a hill and some trees now block your view. This is where you are "flying blind," using only your compass.

The direction you have to travel by compass is 140°. Hold the compass in the palm of your hand with the compass housing turned in such a way that the 140° marking is on the far side of the compass center. Move your feet to rotate your whole body, not just your arms, until you have the compass oriented—that is, until the north part of the compass needle comes to rest pointing at the 360°N marking on the compass housing.

Now sight across the center of the compass and through the 140° marking of the compass housing. Notice some landmark in that direction—a large rock, a prominent tree—and walk to it. Once you reach that spot, take the same bearing toward another landmark. Once there, take the same bearing toward another landmark—and continue in this way until you reach your destination.

Returning to the Original Location

After you have had your fill of exploring around your destination, you are ready for the return journey.

You traveled out in the direction of 140°. To determine the bearing of your return direction—your "back bearing"—add 180° (the number of degrees in a half circle). In this case, the number would be 320°. (If the number of degrees of your original direction had been larger than 180 degrees, you would *subtract* 180° instead of add it.)

Again, remember carefully the number of degrees (320°) of your home journey. As before, jot it down so you don't forget. Then set out for home.

Use your compass as before, holding it in the palm of your hand with the 320° marking on the far side of the compass center. Turn your whole body by moving your feet (don't "corkscrew" your upper body!) until the compass is oriented with the north point of the compass needle pointing to the "North" marking of the compass case, and sight toward the first landmark of your return journey.

If you have been careful in reading your directions and in sighting, you should have no trouble finding your way back safely.

The Modern Orienteering Compass

The modern orienteering compass consists of three basic parts: the magnetic needle, a revolving compass housing, and a transparent

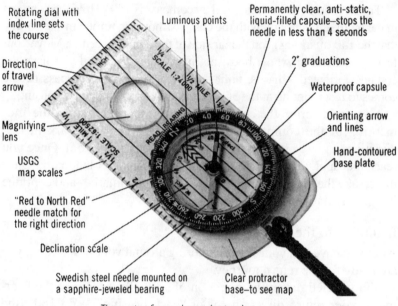

Rotating dial with index line sets the course

Luminous points

Permanently clear, anti-static, liquid-filled capsule—stops the needle in less than 4 seconds

Direction of travel arrow

2° graduations

Waterproof capsule

Magnifying lens

Orienting arrow and lines

USGS map scales

Hand-contoured base plate

"Red to North Red" needle match for the right direction

Declination scale

Swedish steel needle mounted on a sapphire-jeweled bearing

Clear protractor base—to see map

The parts of a modern orienteering compass.

base plate. Each has its own special function, but all three working together make the orienteering compass an efficient and highly practical instrument. While the illustration above will help you gain familiarity, it would be best to buy or borrow an orienteering compass so that you can see how the three parts function.

The *magnetic needle* of the orienteering compass is suspended on a needle-sharp point around which it swings freely on a sapphire bearing. The north end of the needle is painted red—on some models it is also marked with a luminous band.

The rim of the *compass housing* is marked with the initials of the four cardinal points—N (north), E (east), S (south) and W (west)—and is divided into degree lines. Each space between the lines on the housing represents 2 degrees. Every twentieth-degree line is marked by a number—from 20 to 360. The transparent inside bottom of the compass housing is provided with an arrow that points directly to the housing's 360°N marking. This arrow is the *orienting arrow*. The compass is *oriented*—that is, turned so that the north marking of the compass points toward the Magnetic North Pole—whenever the red north end of the magnetic needle lies over the orienting arrow, pointing to the letter "N" on the rim of the housing. In the bottom of the compass housing are engraved several lines that run parallel with the orienting arrow. These lines are the compass's *orienting lines*, also called the magnetic-north lines or compass meridian lines.

The compass housing is attached to a rectangular transparent *base plate* in such a way that it can be easily turned. A line to show direction is engraved in this base plate. It runs from the rim of the compass housing to the front edge of the plate, where it spreads into an arrow, called the *direction-of-travel* arrow. The raised part of the base plate (on which the compass housing moves) has a black index pointer on a white background to show at what degree number the compass housing is set. The side edges of the base plate are parallel to the direction-of-travel arrow line.

The side edge and the front edge of the base plate have markings for measuring. On some models they represent inches and millimeters; on others, the more common map scales. Still other orienteering

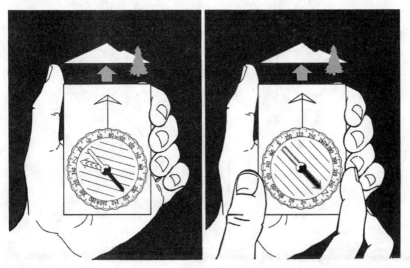

To find a direction with the orienteering compass, point the direction-of-travel arrow to a landmark and turn the housing until the needle lies over the orienting arrow. The bearing to the hill is 225°.

compasses come with interchangeable scales for use with maps of different types.

Finding Bearings with the Orienteering Compass

Finding a bearing with the orienteering compass is a simple matter. Squarely face a distant point or landmark. Hold the orienteering compass level at waist height, or a little higher, with the direction-of-travel arrow pointing straight ahead.

Orient your compass by turning the compass housing without moving the base plate until the compass needle lies over the orienteering

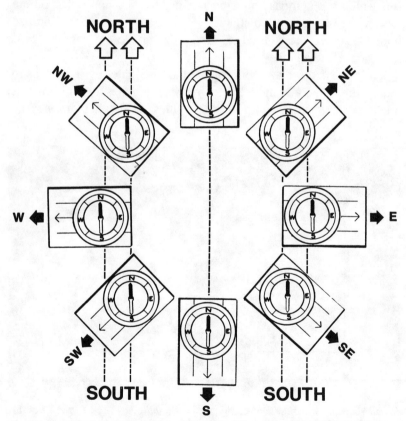

To go in any of the four cardinal and four intercardinal directions, set the base of the direction line at the direction desired, orient the compass, and follow the direction-of-travel arrow.

To go in a certain direction, set the degree number over the index pointer, point the direction-of-travel arrow straight ahead of you, orient the compass, and proceed.

arrow on the inside bottom of the compass housing, with its north part pointing to the letter "N."

Read the bearing (the degree mark of the direction) on the rim of the compass housing at the spot where the black index pointer shows it to be.

It's as easy as that with an orienteering compass—no sighting over the center and outside rim and no chance of an incorrect reading as with the ordinary compass.

Direction-Finding Practice

Before going outdoors, become thoroughly familiar with the use of the compass through indoor practice. Then continue practicing outside. Soon you will have mastered it!

Finding Direction Indoors **Indoor Practice**

Objective To learn how to use the orienteering compass for taking direction bearings.

Test Yourself Stand in the middle of a room. With the orienteering compass, determine ten different directions by the method described on pages

80–81. Examples: from the middle of the room to the doorknob, to the nearest table leg, to the right-hand edge of the window, to the picture on the wall, to the blackboard, and so on.

Group Activity Prepare by marking the floor with as many numbers as there are players (tape down papers with numbers on them, or use chalk, depending on the floor). Then tape similar numbered cards on the walls around the room. Determine the degree readings from each number on the floor to the corresponding number on the wall, and make a list of the "answers."

Each participant should have an orienteering compass, a pencil, and a piece of paper.

The game starts with each participant taking a position over a number on the floor. On the signal "Go," players take the degree reading to the card that bears the same number that they are standing on. They write down that number and the degree bearing it took to get there. When the leader says "Change," each player moves up a number. The first player goes to the number 2 spot, the second player goes to the number 3 spot, and so forth. When all players are in their new positions, another "Go" signal is given, and players take the reading toward the card that bears the number upon which they now stand . . . and so on. The player with the most correct readings within 10 degrees wins.

Relay Activity Divide the players into teams. Instead of marking as many numbers on the floor as there are players, only one number is written per team. On the walls, fasten as many numbered cards as there are players in each relay team. Each team has one orienteering compass to share. On the signal "Go," the first player on each team runs to the team mark on the floor and takes the reading to the card numbered 1. He or she returns and hands off the compass to a second player, who takes a reading to card number 2, and so on. The fastest team with the most correct readings wins.

....

Finding Directions Outdoors ✦ Outdoor Project

Objective Complete familiarity with the use of the orienteering compass to find bearings in the field.

Test Yourself Proceed to a location from which a dozen or more prominent landmarks may be seen (buildings, trees, etc.). With the orienteering compass, determine the compass direction, or bearing, to each of them using the method described on pages 80–81.

Group Activity At a high station point with good visibility, set up a number of markers as described on page 82, with each marker pointing to a prominent landmark. Bring the group to the station and provide each player with an orienteering compass, pencil, and paper. Have each player move clockwise from marker to marker and determine the compass direction toward each of the landmarks to which the markers point. Set a time limit for finishing the project, such as twenty minutes. Score 10 points for each compass direction correct to within 5 degrees.

··

Following a Bearing with the Orienteering Compass

Let's say that you are standing somewhere out in a field and have made up your mind to proceed cross-country to a hilltop in the distance.

Set your orienteering compass for the direction in which the hilltop lies by holding your compass with the direction-of-travel arrow pointing toward your destination. Turn the compass housing until the red north part of the compass needle points to the letter "N" on the rim of the housing. Proceed straight ahead in the direction the direction-of-travel arrow points.

If you lose sight of the distant hilltop, hold the compass in front of you at about chest height, orient it, and sight toward a close-by landmark, perhaps a particular rock or tree that is in the direction the arrow points. Walk to that point, then take a similar reading to the next visible landmark in the correct direction. Keep doing so until you reach your destination. It is very important to remember not to twist the compass housing once you have set the compass for the direction.

What about compass degrees? What about figures to remember? You can forget about compass degrees and figures when you use an orienteering compass, which is one of its great advantages. Your compass is already set. There is nothing to remember; just orient it in the direction you want to go and then proceed.

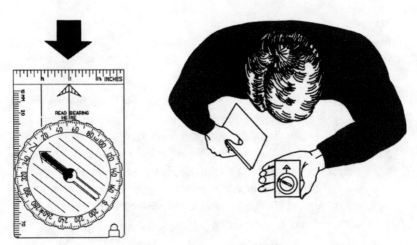

To return home, do not reset the compass. Instead, point the direction-of-travel arrow toward you, orient the compass, and walk against the direction-of-travel arrow.

Returning to the Original Location

You have reached your destination and have decided it is time to return home. Your orienteering compass is already set for your return journey.

When you went out, you held the compass with the direction-of-travel arrow at the front of the base plate pointing *away from you* toward your travel destination.

For your return trip, hold the compass level in the usual manner, but with the direction-of-travel arrow pointing *toward you* instead of away from you. Orient the compass by turning your whole body. Do *not* touch the compass housing! Turn your body until the north end of the needle points to the "N" of the compass housing. Raise your eyes and locate a landmark directly in front of you. Walk to this landmark. Orient the compass again, pick another landmark ahead of you—and so on, until you have returned to your starting point.

Direction-Following Practice

For precision compass work, it is important to be able to follow a compass bearing without reference to any landscape feature—figuratively blindfolded.

Objective Learning to follow a compass bearing with precision.

Test Yourself Go to an open field and place a stake or other marker in the ground. Starting from that point, set your orienteering compass at any bearing you desire. Place a large paper bag over your head, folding its edge so you can see the compass being held at waist height, but cannot see ahead. You may look silly, but you will be learning a valuable skill!

Turn around three times, then orient the compass and walk 50 steps in the direction set on it. Turn the compass for the return journey, as explained on page 84, with the direction-of-travel arrow pointing toward you. Walk 45 steps using that back bearing. You should end up within less than 10 feet from your stake, or starting point.

Group Activity Set up half as many numbered stakes as there are players, 5 feet apart in a north-south line. Divide the players into two teams and place a player from each team at each stake. Have the players from one team set their compasses at bearings between 45° and 115°. The other team should set theirs between 225° and 315°. Each player, head covered with a paper bag and compass in hand, turns around three times, follows the compass bearing for 50 steps, then turns and follows the back bearing back for 45 steps. Only players ending up within 10 steps of their starting point score. The team with the most scores wins.

Test Your Compass Skills

So far your compass work has been elementary practice. It is now time for you to get into the field for some more comprehensive compass work, so grab your compass and test your skills.

A Three-Legged Compass Walk

Try a simple compass walk over a short distance to see how you do.

Are you ready to gamble a quarter on your compass skills? No? Well, then make it a nickel. Place a nickel on the ground between

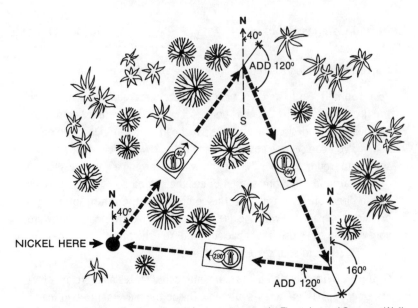

For simple practice in using the orienteering compass, try the Three-Legged Compass Walk. Place a marker and add 120° to each setting from the original.

your feet. Set the compass for an arbitrary direction between 0 and 120° by twisting the compass housing until the black index pointer on the rim is at the degree number you have decided on. We'll use 40° as an example, setting the compass for traveling in the direction of 40°.

Hold the compass level at about waist height with the direction-of-travel arrow straight ahead. Move your body by moving your feet (don't just twist your upper body!) until the compass needle is oriented, with the north part of the needle pointing to the "N" of the compass housing. Look up and decide on a landmark of some sort directly ahead of you in the 40° direction. Walk straight toward the landmark without looking at your compass for 40 steps (about 100 feet). Stop.

Look at your compass again. Add 120° to your original 40°, making it 160°. Reset your compass housing so that the index pointer is now at the 160° marking. Again, hold the compass flat before you, with the direction-of-travel arrow pointing straight ahead. Move your whole body until the compass needle lies over the orienting arrow in the housing, with the north part pointing to "N." Again, look up, pick a landmark in the direction of 160°, and walk toward it 40 steps. Stop.

Again, add 120° to your setting of 160°, making it 280°. Reset your compass, determine the direction to walk, and take 40 steps in the direction toward which the direction-of-travel arrow points. Stop. Bend down and pick up your nickel! The nickel should be right at your feet if your compass readings and your walking were precise.

How come? Look at the diagram on page 86. You have been walking the three sides of an equilateral triangle. When you finish, you should be right back at your starting point.

Try this exercise a couple of times, each time starting out with a degree setting somewhere between 0 and 120°.

Now that you have the idea, you'll realize you don't really need to stick to a starting direction between 0 and 120°. That was done for the sake of simplicity. You can pick any number of degrees that you want. You then have to remember that any time you are adding and you arrive at a figure larger than 360°, you must subtract 360° from it to get to your next direction. As an example, if your first direction is 225°, your second is 225° plus 120°, or 345°. Your third would be 345° plus 120°, or 465°. There is no such figure on a compass, so you subtract 360° and get 105°, your correct third direction.

A mini-orienteering walk gives excellent training in using a compass. Such a course can be set up in a small area, accessible to all.

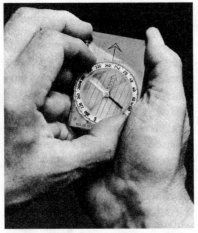

To follow degree specified, set the number over the index pointer...

... point direction-of-travel arrow ahead, orient compass, proceed.

Outdoor Direction Project

When you have gotten comfortable with your orienteering compass, try these simple exercises.

Silver Dollar Hunt   **Outdoor Project**

Objective Practice in taking and following degree bearings.

Group Activity The Silver Dollar Hunt is the Three-Legged Compass Walk described on pages 85–87 turned into a project for a small or medium-size group, such as a Scout patrol. Make up as many "silver dollars" (2- to 3-inch lids cut from tin cans or plastic potato chip lids make great ones!) as there are participants, and a number of instruction cards with distances and directions like these:

"40 steps 90°—40 steps 210°—40 steps 330°"
"50 steps 45°—50 steps 165°—50 steps 285°"
"45 steps 18°—45 steps 138°—45 steps 258°"

(Notice that the distances are alike on each card, and that the directions start with a degree bearing of less than 120°, to which 120° is added, then another 120°. The explanation and illustration for this are on pages 86–87.)

Scatter the participants over a field with fairly tall grass or in a wooded terrain with some underbrush, if possible. Place a "silver dollar" at the feet of each player. On a signal, each player takes the first bearing on his or her card, walks the first distance and then stops. When all have stopped, give the next signal. Each player then takes the second bearing indicated on his or her card, walks the second distance, and stops. On the third signal, all walk the third distance indicated and stop. On the fourth and last signal, all the participants bend down and pick up the "silver dollar," which should be at their feet, if the exercise has been done properly. The players who can pick up the silver dollar from their ending position score 100 points.

Schoolyard Compass Game   Outdoor Project

Objective Practice in setting the compass for degree bearings and following them with precision (game devised by Allan Foster).

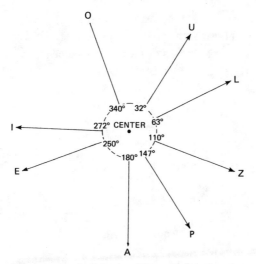

The course for the Schoolyard Compass Game consists of eight stakes placed at the same distance but at different compass bearings from a center stake.

Group Activity The course for this game can be set up in a schoolyard, a playground, a park, or a Scout camp. The course consists of eight marked stakes set up in a large circle. The stakes are marked with the letters I, O, U, L, Z, P, A, and E. For laying out the course you will also need an unmarked center stake, a string 50 feet long or longer, and an orienteering compass.

To lay out the course, place the unmarked stake in the center of the area you have chosen for the game. Attach the measuring string to this center stake. Starting from the center stake each time, set the compass bearing as indicated in the illustration on page 89. Stretch out the measuring string along this bearing and place the respective marked stake at the end of the string. The success of the game depends on the careful positioning of these markers.

To play the game, each participant is provided with an orienteering compass, a pencil, and an instruction card. The card specifies at what marked stake to start and gives instruction to follow five compass bearings from marker to marker around the course. You will find the instructions below for the cards and ten players. If your group is larger, run the participants in sections.

When ready to start, each participant goes to the marker that has the letter that corresponds to the starting point of his or her instruction card and proceeds according to the instructions. The player copies down on the card the letter on each marker on the route. When finished, each player turns the card over to the judge. The six-letter code produced, beginning with the starting-stake letter, is then checked against the correct letter sequence as it is found on page 91.

1. Start at stake marked A
    - Proceed 305°, 29°, 100°, 162°, 221°
    - Markers reached: _____
2. Start at stake marked E
    - Proceed 358°, 68°,140°,198°, 252°
    - Markers reached: _____
3. Start at stake marked I
    - Proceed 42°, 112°, 178°, 236°, 305°
    - Markers reached: _____
4. Start at stake marked O
    - Proceed 100°, 162°, 221°, 287°, 358°
    - Markers reached: _____

5. Start at stake marked   U
   - Proceed 140°, 198°, 252°, 320°, 42°
   - Markers reached: _____
6. Start at stake marked   L
   - Proceed 178°, 236°, 305°, 29°, 100°
   - Markers reached: _____
7. Start at stake marked   Z
   - Proceed 221°, 287°, 358°, 68°, 140°
   - Markers reached: _____
8. Start at stake marked   P
   - Proceed 252°, 320°, 42°, 112°, 178°
   - Markers reached: _____
9. Start at stake markedE   A
   - Proceed 320°, 68°, 162°, 236°, 305°
   - Markers reached: _____
10. Start at stake marked   E
   - Proceed 29°, 112°, 198°, 287°, 358°
   - Markers reached: _____

(Correct answers can be found on pages 224–225.)

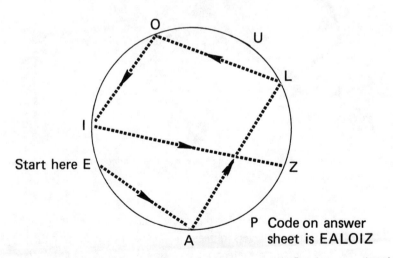

A player in the Schoolyard Compass Game is told to start at stake E and to proceed 125°, 26°, 292°, 222°, 106°. The answering code would be EALOIZ.

Mini-Orienteering Compass Walk

Objective The Mini-Orienteering Compass Walk covers an area of only a few hundred yards, yet provides an excellent training opportunity in walking cross-country by compass. It can easily be set up on the property around a school, at a Scout camp, or in a local park, as long as there are trees.

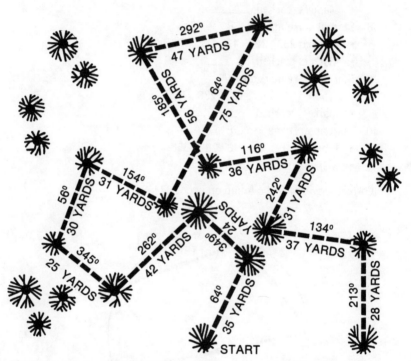

A typical course for a Mini-Orienteering Walk. It can be arranged in a school playground area, at a Scout camp site, or in a local park.

Group Activity The course for this game is laid in wooded territory by attaching a series of markers to trees. Each marker has its own identifying number, and contains the direction and distance to the next marked tree.

It is best to have two people working together setting up the course, each with a marker pen. You can use a piece of paper or a paper plate as a marker, and tack it gently to the tree. Do your best not to damage the tree, and be sure to clean up after you are finished.

Place the first marker, labeled with the number "1," on the first tree, and decide upon a compass bearing. Write the degree number on the marker. Then, leaving your helper at Post 1, proceed in the direction you wrote on marker 1 and measure the distance by your steps until you reach another tree that can become your next post. Yell the distance you just walked back to your helper, who writes this distance on the first marker. The marker on the tree now is labeled with which marker it is (1), which bearing to take to the next marker, and the distance away that marker can be found.

Your helper now joins you at Post 2. Put up the next marker, preferably on the back of the tree so that it cannot be seen as you approach. Write the new number (2) and a new bearing on the marker. Follow this bearing until you decide on the location of Post 3, and so on. When you have about a dozen posts scattered among the trees, you are set.

The participants are started at two-minute intervals, each with an orienteering compass. The one with the fastest time around the course wins.

Mini-Orienteering Walk provides training in walking cross-country by compass. Very little space is required for putting up an effective course.

Objective To practice following compass bearings and measuring distances by walking. This type of compass competition/training is particularly suited for school grounds and campsites. The course can be set up quickly and can remain in location, so that large numbers of pupils or campers can try their compass skills under the direct guidance of their teacher or leader (devised by Elston F. Larson).

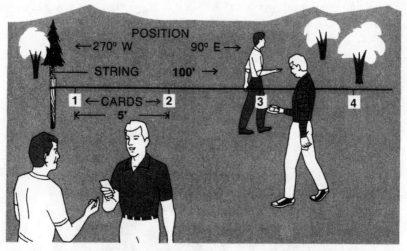

It takes only a string 100 feet long, plus extra for tying, marked with tags at 5-foot intervals, to set up a Compass Competition for school grounds or a campsite.

Group Activity Before the start of this compass training competition, each participant needs to know the length of his or her step. Mark off a distance of 200 feet on the ground, so that people can measure the length of their step, as described on pages 55–56.

The course for this exercise consists of twenty markers, numbered 1 through 20, placed 5 feet apart on a straight magnetic east-west line. The easiest way to do this is to tie a loop at each end of some twine or other strong cord, 100 feet apart. Stretch the cord between two pegs in the east-west direction, with a tag labeled with number 1 on the west end. Tie the other tags, totaling twenty, to the cord at 5-foot intervals.

When ready to start, each participant is provided with an orienteering compass and an instruction card specifying at which marker to start and how to proceed. A set of instructions for ten players follows. If your group is larger than ten, you can run the participants in several sections, or run it like a relay, where teammates hand off the compass and directions as they finish the course.

Each participant goes to the marker that has the number that corresponds with the starting point on his or her card, and follows the instructions. When finished, each writes down the number of the marker nearest to the destination reached (all the routes lead back to markers on the course line), and turns it in to the judge. The correct destination for each of the starting points can be found on page 225.

A player reaching the correct destination receives a score of 100 points. For each foot of error the judge deducts 1 point. For incorrect markers, 5 points are subtracted.

Run the game three times with different starting points for a possible maximum score of 300 points.

Start at Point 1.
- Go 36° for 122 feet.
- Then 149° for 58 feet.
- Then 235° for 86 feet.
Destination reached: No. _____

Start at Point 2.
- Go 17° for 104 feet.
- Then 150° for 52 feet.
- Then 142° for 64 feet.
Destination reached: No. _____

Start at Point 3.
- Go 38° for 125 feet.
- Then 237° for 90 feet.
- Then 186° for 50 feet.
Destination reached: No. _____

Start at Point 4.
- Go 36° for 122 feet.
- Then 174° for 50 feet.

- Then 228° for 74 feet.

Destination reached: No. _____

Start at Point 5.
- Go 22° for 107 feet.
- Then 158° for 54 feet.
- Then 186° for 50 feet.

Destination reached: No. _____

Start at Point 6.
- Go 3° for 100 feet.
- Then 132° for 74 feet.
- Then 225° for 69 feet.

Destination reached: No. _____

Start at Point 7.
- Go 34° for 119 feet.
- Then 186° for 50 feet.
- Then 228° for 74 feet.

Destination reached: No. _____

Start at Point 8.
- Go 346° for 102 feet.
- Then 129° for 78 feet.
- Then 211° for 58 feet.

Destination reached: No. _____

Start at Point 9.
- Go 346° for 102 feet.
- Then 129° for 78 feet.
- Then 186° for 50 feet.

Destination reached: No. _____

Start at Point 10.
- Go 343° for 104 feet.
- Then 141° for 64 feet.
- Then 145° for 61 feet.

Destination reached: No. _____

••

Objective To practice following a cross-country bearing with precision.

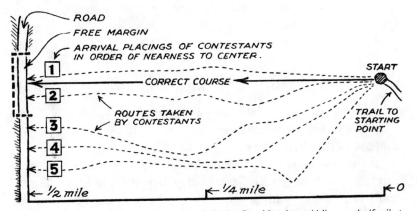

To lay out a Compass Walk course, set out from the Free Margin and hike one-half mile to mark the starting point. Contestants begin at Start and must hit inside the Free Margin.

Group Activity After some practice using the compass, plan a beeline compass walk over a distance of approximately one-half mile. To lay out the course, locate a stretch of straight road lined with fence posts or find a straight stretch along a field or other open area and put up your own stakes. Tack markers numbered 1 through 10 on ten of these posts about a hundred feet apart.

At one of these markers—number 4, for example—face the line of posts at a right angle. Proceed in that direction as carefully as possible for half a mile, or about fifteen minutes.

Place a marker here. This is a starting point for the players. Then add 180° to your bearing if it is below 180°, or subtract 180° from it if is above 180°. This is your back bearing, the direction from the point where you now are to the post from which you started. It is also the bearing that the participants are to follow to reach their correct destination.

Each player is given an orienteering compass and a bearing to follow. On a half-mile course, a margin of error of 100 feet can be allowed. Thus, if your original starting post was number 4, hitting the markers between 3 and 5 scores a possible 100 points.

The illustration on page 97 shows an example of where five partici-pants ended up after starting at the same place and trying to reach the same destination. The solid arrow shows the correct course. Contestants one and two would both get 100 points, but the first contestant was clos-est to the correct course.

<hr/>

A Beeline Out-and-Back Compass Walk

After you have mastered the use of the compass with a fair degree of accuracy over short distances, you are ready for a cross-country compass walk called a "beeline" walk.

Take yourself out to some fairly familiar terrain—your local park, your base camp, or some other countryside you know. This is not the time to be too adventurous! Decide on the compass direction you would like to follow. A half an hour's walk out would be about a mile, with about the same length of time to get back.

When you have arrived at your starting point, set the compass for the number of degrees you have decided on. Then determine the first leg of your journey in a way you should be comfortable with by now:

1. Hold the compass level before you, with the direction-of-travel arrow pointing straight ahead.
2. Turn your whole body, including your feet, until the compass needle lies directly over the orienting arrow inside the com-pass housing, north end toward N.
3. Look up and decide on a landmark in the direction in which you are sighting.
4. Proceed to the landmark without looking at the compass.

When you have reached your first landmark and thus have com-pleted the first lap of your beeline walk, sight, in the same way, toward the next landmark in the direction in which you are traveling.

If you come across an obstacle such as a pond, a swamp, a fence, or other obstruction, you'll have to read the next section! Presume for this exercise that you can keep walking.

Eventually, you will have reached the distance and length of time that you had decided on, and you are ready for the return journey.

Turn around and travel back as described on page 84. Hold the compass level in your hand in the usual manner, but with the direction-of-travel arrow pointing toward you instead of away from you. Turn your whole body until your compass is oriented with the north end of the needle pointing at N, raise your eyes, and pick the first landmark for your return trip. When you reach that landmark, use your compass to orient yourself to the next one, until you are safely back where you started.

Overcoming Obstacles

On a cross-country walk there will probably be occasions when there is an obstacle—a lake, a swamp, a building, private property, or other feature in your way. If you can't walk through or over the obstacle, you'll have to figure out how to walk around it.

If you can see across or through your obstacle, it's a relatively simple matter. Locate a prominent landmark on the other side of the

If you run up against an obstacle that you can see across, pick a prominent landmark on the opposite side of the obstacle and proceed to it.

obstacle, such as a large tree or a building. Walk to it by going around your obstacle, and take your next bearing, as usual, from there.

Before setting out again, make certain you are on the right track by taking a back-reading. Look back toward the point from which you came. That point should be directly (a half circle) behind you. You could reset your compass for a back-reading by adding 180 degrees to the compass setting if it is below 180 degrees, or by subtracting 180 degrees if the setting is above 180 degrees. But rather than complicating matters for yourself by adding or subtracting and later

After having walked around your obstacle, take a back-reading toward the point from which you started, to make certain of your course.

resetting to your original degree number, make use of your direction-of-travel arrow on the base plate of your orienteering compass.

Do not change the setting of the compass! Simply hold the orienteering compass backward, with the direction-of-travel arrow pointing toward you instead of away from you. Orient the compass in the usual way with the north part of the needle at N. Then sight against the direction-of-travel arrow, instead of with it, and raise your eyes. You should be looking directly back toward the point from which you came.

If you can't see across or through the obstacle, you can walk around it by right angles. Turn at a right angle from your route and, counting your steps, walk until you are certain you are beyond the extension of the obstacle in that direction. Then turn at a right angle back on your original bearing, and proceed until you are clear of the obstacle. Again, turn at a right angle back toward your original sighting line, and step off the identical number of steps you took during your first direction change. You are now back on your original sighting line. Make another right-angle turn and proceed in your original direction.

You can, of course, make these right-angle turns by resetting the compass at each turn, adding 90 degrees for each turn to the right or subtracting 90 degrees for each turn to the left from the original compass setting. But why do it the hard way when you can do it without any resetting whatsoever? You can do it by taking advantage of the right angles of the orienteering compass's base plate.

Let us say that we want to *go to the right around the obstacle ahead*. For your first right-angle turn, hold your orienteering compass with the base plate crosswise in your hand, with the direction-of-travel arrow pointing toward your left. Orient the compass in the usual manner. Sight along the back edge of the base plate, from left corner to right corner toward a suitable landmark. Walk enough steps (count them!) toward the landmark to be certain that you are beyond the obstacle in that direction. How can you be certain? You can't really know until you use your map and compass together, but you can make an educated guess by looking at the terrain and other physical features.

For the second turn (to the left), hold the compass in the usual way, with the direction-of-travel arrow pointing straight ahead of you. You are back on the original bearing. Walk far enough to get well beyond your obstacle in this direction. The illustration on page 102 should help clarify what you are undertaking.

For the third turn (again to the left), hold the compass with the base plate *crosswise* again, but with the direction-of-travel arrow to your *right*. You orient the compass and sight along the back edge of the base plate, this time from right corner to left corner. Walk in the new direction exactly the same number of steps you took in your first direction change.

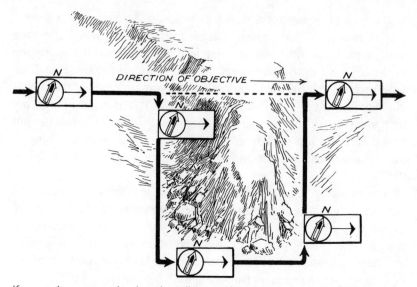

If you can't see across the obstacle, walk around it at right angles, using the back edge of the orienteering compass's base plate for sighting.

For your final turn, to the right, orient the compass with the direction-of-travel arrow pointing directly in front of you. The obstacle has been overcome and you continue walking toward your initial destination.

If, instead of going to the right to get around the obstacle, it seems more convenient to *go to the left around it*, reverse these instructions. First, hold the base plate with the direction-of-travel arrow pointing to the left for the first turn and to the right for the third turn.

Fishing and Hunting: Special Use of Your Compass

Exploring the world around you with a compass as your guide is a fun and exciting experience. You may even choose to try the sport of orienteering, which we will introduce you to shortly. But if you enjoy fishing and hunting, you can also put your orienteering compass to a number of other uses.

Finding a Choice Fishing Lake

Let's say you are on the lookout for the best possible trout stream or lake. What fisherman isn't? You have been hearing about Silver Lake from some other anglers and would love to give it a try. Silver Lake, your friends tell you, is located directly southwest of the Blackton railway station. But there is no road from the train station to the lake. You'll have to find your way cross-country.

One beautiful morning, you arrive at Blackton station. Finding the lake will be simple with your orienteering compass.

You know you have to travel southwest. That would be 225°. Set your compass for 225° by lining up the 225° mark on the compass housing over the black index pointer of the rim. Compass in hand, direction-of-travel arrow pointing straight ahead, you orient the compass and sight. According to your friends, Silver Lake lies in that direction. You reach it without difficulty and enjoy a great day of fishing!

When you are ready to return to Blackton station, simply back-track by compass, as described on page 84. Sight over your compass, but with the base plate's direction-of-travel arrow pointing toward you instead of away from you. Now get those fish home!

Getting to a wonderful fishing lake and back can be easy with an orienteering compass.

Relocating a Top Fishing Spot

Fishing along the shore of Silver Lake has been fun, and you've caught some nice fish. But the "big ones," they tell you, are way out in the depths of the lake. One day you get a boat and try your luck. After a cast or two, you nab a big one! You anchor the boat and keep on fishing. That first one wasn't just luck; you've found your spot and keep catching some beauties until you've reached your limit.

Obviously, you've found a place you want to remember and return to. Even though it is out in the middle of a great big lake, you will be able to find your exact location again by using your orienteering compass. It is simply a matter of taking some cross-bearings, writing them down, and using those notes next time you want to find this spot.

To take cross-bearings, pick out two prominent and permanent landmarks on land and determine the directions to them. Choose your landmarks carefully. The large white house may be painted red the next time you come and the large tree may have been cut down. A large cliff or rock or perhaps a boat dock would be better.

To find the bearing to the cliff, point the direction-of-travel arrow toward the cliff and turn the compass housing until the compass is

When you've found an especially good fishing spot in a lake, make notes of cross-bearings to two landmarks; use them to find the same spot next time.

oriented—until the north part of the needle points to N. Read the number of degrees on the edge of the compass housing at the base of the direction line. Let's say it is 113°.

Next point the direction-of-travel arrow toward the second landmark, the boat dock. Orient the compass. Let's say the reading to the dock is 32°.

Write down in your notebook something like: "Excellent fishing spot, Silver Lake, 113° to cliff, 32° to boat dock." The next time you decide to go fishing, rent the boat, get out your notes, and set out.

The direction from the fishing spot to the dock was 32°. Obviously, then, the direction from the dock to the fishing spot would be a half circle

Don't forget to learn how to use your compass to return to a prized fishing spot . . . and don't forget to learn how to get safely back home.

the other way. Therefore you add 180° to the 32°, making it 212°. (If the original figure had been larger than 180°, you would subtract 180° instead of add it.) Set your compass by turning the compass housing until the 212° mark is located directly over the black index pointer of the rim. Point the direction-of-travel arrow straight over the bow of your boat and have your friend turn the boat until the north part of the compass needle points to N. Raise your head and locate a landmark on the opposite shore—let's say a rock—and have your friend steer the boat directly toward it.

Now reset your compass to 113°—the reading toward the cliff. Orient the compass in your hand, north part of the needle on N, and continue sighting over the direction-of-travel arrow while your friend goes on guiding the boat toward the rock.

You are almost there. When the arrow hits the cliff, you've made it. Set your anchor, throw in the line, and catch those fish—we hope!

Using the Compass for Hunting

The orienteering compass can also come in handy for the hunter. Let's say you want to hunt in a northwesterly direction from your camp, since there were plenty of deer that way last year.

You got your deer—now to get help bringing it out. Follow your orienteering compass to the nearest road, and later backtrack with the same compass setting.

Set the compass at northwest—that would be 315°—by turning the compass housing until the 315° mark is over the black index pointer of the rim. Hold the compass with the direction-of-travel arrow pointing straight ahead, and orient the compass with the north part of the needle toward N. The arrow points the way you want to go. As you walk, check your compass now and then to be sure you are continuing in the general direction you chose.

When you feel you've had enough hunting for the day and want to return to camp, check your direction again, but backtrack as explained on page 84.

Finding Your Kill

Let's say that someday you may be in real luck and you get that long-anticipated ten-point buck you have been dreaming about . . . or another large, heavy quarry. You have to get it back to camp, but cannot handle the heavy beast alone. You need to get help, but finding the exact location could be very challenging—unless you use your orienteering compass.

Plan your strategy. You know from your general knowledge of the lay of the land that there is a road a half mile or so south-east that leads to the hunting lodge where you should be able to get help.

Mark the buck with something easily seen from a distance—a white handkerchief tied to a nearby tree would do, if it isn't snowing!

Set your compass for south-east (13°) to find that road, and start off, accurately following the direction-of-travel arrow. Pick out landmarks on the line of travel and proceed from landmark to landmark. Count your double-steps carefully as you go, to be sure of the distance.

You reach the road after 512 double-steps. Mark the spot clearly with some dead limbs, a log, or pile of rocks, whatever you can be sure to recognize later when you return.

After you find some help, and maybe even a packhorse or a four-wheeler, you travel back up the road until you find your marker.

Now it's a matter of backtracking until you find your buck. Your compass is already set, since you have not changed the setting. All you have to do is follow the compass in the opposite direction by sighting against the direction-of-travel arrow instead of with it. Go from landmark to landmark and count off those 512 double-steps. Where is your deer? You probably won't be right on top of it, but you'll be close. Mark the point you reached, and start circling it in an ever-widening spiral. You should see the handkerchief in the tree . . . and the buck. Now you can really brag to your friends!

PART 3

ADVENTURE

Fun with Map and Compass

While living in Sweden in the 1950s, I was invited by some American friends to join them for a hunting trip in the Four Corners region of Colorado, Utah, New Mexico, and Arizona. Although hunting is popular in Scandinavia (especially moose!), I had never been interested in the sport. Nevertheless, I accepted the invitation, welcoming the opportunity to enjoy the magnificent wilderness of the area.

While my friends left camp every day with their rifles, I used a topographic map to plan long hikes to a variety of interesting places, including Indian rock dwellings and mountaintops that promised wide vistas of the American West. On one of these climbs up a mountain, I found an Indian arrowhead, a beautiful artifact chiseled from snow-white quartz.

It wasn't long before my American friends started to tease me, saying I had no idea how to track a deer or even get a good shot at one. My ego eventually got the best of me and I gave in. I left shortly after lunch one day for an area where no one in our party had hunted yet, but it was difficult keeping my thoughts from wandering to the beauty of the landscape and its vibrant fall colors.

I hadn't anticipated coming across a deer so quickly. Yet only an hour or so from camp, I spotted one near a small clearing and took aim. BANG . . . bang, bang, bang! The shot from my rifle echoed through the mountains. It was my first shot ever at any living creature . . . and my last.

Now what? I walked toward the deer and found I had my first kill. It was a big buck with impressive antlers, a trophy rack even an accomplished hunter would be proud of. But my fleeting sense of accomplishment quickly gave way to sadness. A clap of thunder jolted me to my senses, and I started thinking about how to get help to bring the deer back to camp.

I carefully retraced my route in my mind. Upon leaving camp, I had followed a trail that ran north-south for about one-half mile. Then I'd strolled east into the woods for thirty minutes before turning south, traveling parallel with the original trail. I figured I had walked south about one mile. It should be easy, I thought, to reach the trail by walking due west.

As the thunderstorm hit, it started to snow! I had never experienced such unusual weather conditions. If I was ever going to find the area again, I'd have to mark it clearly. First, I broke tree limbs to form a circle around the deer. I also broke branches in a straight line—about twenty-five feet to both sides of the deer—perpendicular to the westerly path I planned to take back to the trail. This line was to function as a catching feature on my return to guide me to the buck.

After setting my orienteering compass on west, I started hiking to the trail. Along the way, I broke more branches as markers and counted my paces so I would know how far into the woods the deer was positioned. I tried to keep in a straight westerly direction so it would be easier to follow the markings back. After 260 paces, I reached the trail and marked the spot.

The snow was already two or three inches deep and still falling. I rushed back to the camp, arriving just before nightfall. I had trouble convincing my friends that there was any chance of finding my kill in the storm, but one of them finally agreed to come along. We saddled two horses and left.

I wasn't an experienced horseman, so I had a tough time keeping up with my friend. In the growing darkness, we passed my markings on the trail. Fortunately, I recognized a few easily identifiable features just north of the spot, and we turned back.

After dismounting the horses, I set the compass on east—opposite the westerly direction I had walked from the kill to the trail. I counted my paces as we walked, looking for my broken branches. It was dark now, and the snow was about four inches deep. We had to use flashlights to follow the direction indicated by the compass and the broken branches.

When we had covered 225 of the 260 paces, we started to look carefully for the branch markers around the deer. There was no trace. My friend wanted to give up. Suddenly, at about 270 steps, I spotted the antlers, poking up from the snow like fallen branches.

We had no problem finding our way back to the trail and the camp. There, my navigation skills became the talk around the campfire for days. All of my hunting buddies decided they would get a compass when they returned home.

They were smart. A compass is a must for every outdoor enthusiast, with or without a map. It puts the "invisible power of direction," Earth's magnetism, at your fingertips.

—**Björn Kjellström**

The Excitement of the Uncertain

Now that you know the function of the map and compass separately, you will want to use them together to find your way, and, possibly, for your first taste of orienteering. This thrilling sport tests the art of traveling through unknown territory with a map and a compass, and is the best way to practice navigation through the woods.

Using a map and compass will open the door to your enjoyment of nature. You will increase the fun of your outings as your trips take you cross-country, off the beaten track, away from the "been there, done that" to places you've never been. With new things to see and to experience, there will also be the excitement of the uncertain: "Am I on the right trail?" "Will I hit the tip of the lake, as planned?" "Can I get through the swamp, or do I have to pick another route?" "Are we there yet?"

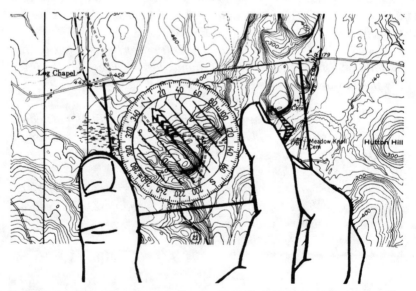

First step *in setting your compass by the map: Place the base plate on the map in such a way that one edge of it connects your starting point to your destination.*

Maps and Compasses Are Made to Work Together

Even though you have been taught through this book to use a map without a compass, and a compass without a map, your biggest achievement will be in using them together. Only under certain limited situations can you use them with success independently. The history of mapmaking tells us that good maps were not made until the mapmakers started to use the compass to get exact orienteering lines—the meridians. A compass is not much use by itself unless you have a map, at least in your mind.

When you begin to use a map and compass together, you may want to do some hiking and orienteering on your own. Please keep safety foremost in your mind. You can bring a cell phone and a GPS, but there are conditions under which neither may function. Taking along a buddy is a good idea. Always tell somebody—a friend, a park ranger—where you are headed and about what time you expect to be back. Leaving a note in your car window with this information, your cell phone number, and an emergency contact is a smart thing to do. Even the most experienced outdoorsmen can be hit with bad luck and need help!

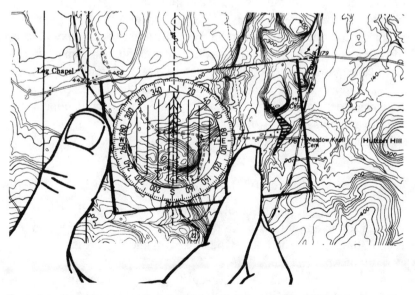

Second step *in setting your compass by the map: Turn the housing until the orienting arrow lies parallel with the nearest meridian. The compass is now set.*

Try orienteering with a club or join other orienteers in a competition. It's a great way to have fun and to get the best practice you can for exploring the out-of-doors by map and compass. Competitive orienteering can, of course, be your goal, but it can also ready you for backpacking, hunting, cross-country skiing, or any other activity you have planned.

Different Kinds of Maps Require Different Techniques

Generally speaking, if you have learned how to read and interpret one kind of map, you can handle them all. But the technique in traveling by a regular topographic map or by a special orienteering map is quite different. When you use a regular topographic map, you have to rely heavily on the proper use of the compass. You have to take and follow compass bearings quite often and sometimes for fairly long distances.

When you navigate through the woods with a special orienteering map, which gives so much more detail in its representation of the terrain, the compass becomes more of a helping tool, especially in an area with lots of small features identifiable on the map. You use the compass primarily to orient, or set, the map. With the highly detailed orienteering map, you can literally follow your route on the map step by step.

Let's examine the principles in using the common topographic map with a compass. For reference purposes, we will be using a protractor-type orienteering compass, such as those originally made popular by the Silva compass. Some of these principles will also apply to the use of an orienteering map, but the differences will be explained later.

Your First Orienteering Trip—at Home

Before you set out on an actual orienteering trip in the field, let's see what is involved by taking the trip at home first, using the training map in the back of the book. Open the map and lay a route on it that you might want to take.

As an example, let's say you want to start your trip at the crossroads ¼ inch southeast of the letter "l" in Log Chapel. According to our map-reading shorthand, that would be: ¼" SE "l" in Log Chapel.

A short, suitable expedition might then take in the road-T north of Meadow Knoll Cemetery, the farmhouse west of Niger Marsh, the crossroads north of the Log Chapel, and back to your starting point, as on the map on page 112.

Setting Your Compass

Pretending you are actually at your starting point, the first thing you would do is orient your map. You have learned to do this by inspection (pages 53–54), by twisting the map around until the landmarks of the map are aligned with the landmarks of your surroundings. Next, you study the map to see what you should expect on the first leg of your journey. If there is an easily identifiable landmark in sight and marked on your map, you could head there. For the sake of this exercise, we'll say there are no easily identifiable terrain features along the route to your destination. You decide to walk straight through, a "beeline" walk.

Your next job is to set your orienteering compass for the first leg of the journey—from the crossroads southeast of Log Chapel to the road-T 13/8 inches northwest of the "H" in Hutton Hill.

You have probably already bought yourself an orienteering compass if you are still reading this book. This is where it gets a workout, as we identify the various compass settings you will use on your hike. When you have a planned route such as this, do all the figuring of compass bearing degrees before you start hiking. It is easier to plan it out on a flat surface like a table.

Place the compass on the training map with one side of the base plate connecting the starting point at the crossroads with your first destination at the road-T and with the direction-of-travel arrow pointing in the direction you intend to go.

Now twist the compass housing until the orienting arrow on the inside of the housing lies parallel to the nearest north line—meridian—of the map, with the north point up.

Your orienteering compass is now set to guide you for your first leg. What is the setting? Check the degree number at the point of the compass housing touched by the direction line. Is it 84°? Correct. By orienting the actual compass in the field, then following the direction-of-travel arrow, you should have no difficulty hitting your first destination.

Next leg: from the road-T to the farmhouse ¾ inches west of the "N" in Niger Marsh. Again, place the compass on the map with the side edge of the base plate connecting the two points. Twist the compass housing until the orienting arrow lies parallel with a map north line, with north to the top. Your compass is set for your next leg. How many degrees?

Next, set the compass from the farmhouse west of Niger Marsh to the crossroads 1⅛ inches north of the "l" in Log Chapel, and finally, for the leg from the crossroads back to the point from which you started.

Your Distances

You now have the compass settings you will use on your way, but there is something else that is important: the distances to be traveled.

Go over your route again to find the most direct (as the crow flies) distances between your different points. Use the inch rule along the side edge of the base plate of your compass. The training map is in the scale of 1:24,000. Each inch, therefore, is 2,000 feet. In measuring, you should get these results:

- Crossroads to road-T N Meadow Knoll Cemetery   7,100 feet
- Road-T to farm W Niger Marsh   2,700 feet
- Farm to crossroads N Log Chapel   7,300 feet
- Crossroads to starting point   2,700 feet
- **Total distance**   **19,800 feet**

Your route, as the crow flies, is 19,800 feet, or a distance of about 3¾ miles. You shouldn't have too much trouble covering this loop in around two hours, unless you encounter unexpected obstacles.

Indoor Map and Compass Practice

Use your compass and the training map to practice some imaginary hikes until setting your compass by map becomes second nature to you.

Objective　To become familiar with setting the orienteering compass for different directions on the map.

Test Yourself　Open up the training map and take out your compass. Locate the crossroads one-quarter inch southeast of the letter "I" in Log Chapel. That is your starting point. Now determine the degree bearings to the following points:

1. Starting point to Post 1, at church 5/8 inch north-northwest of "M" in Meadow Knoll Cemetery _____ °
2. From Post 1 to Post 2, located at road-T 11/16 inch W of "N" in Niger Marsh _____ °
3. From Post 2 to Post 3, at farmhouse 1½ inches NW of "H" in Huckleberry Mtn _____ °

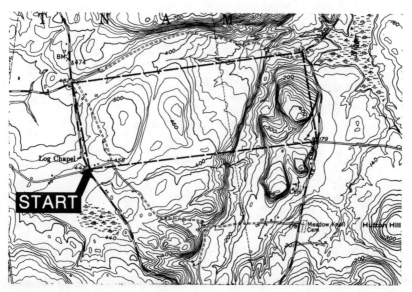

Open up the training map in the back of the book, and locate the territory of the route shown above, the trip described on pages 114–116.

4. From Post 3 to Post 4, barn 3/8 inch NW of "B" in Charter Brook _____°
5. From Post 4 to Goal, at road-T ¼ inch N of "k" in Sucker Brook _____°

(Check your readings against the answers on page 225.)

Just for Fun Each player is provided with a compass, a pencil, and a copy of the training map and the list above. On a given signal, the players determine the bearings. The player who finishes with the most correct answers in the shortest amount of time wins.

···

What Do You Find?

Indoor Practice

··· ···

Objective To practice making correct measurements and to determine compass bearings on the map.

Test Yourself Using the training map and compass, determine the landscape features located at these points:

1. Distance: 2,400 feet.
   Direction: 298° from "H" in Hutton Hill _____
2. Distance: 4,000 feet.
   Direction: 182° from "R" in Record Hill _____
3. Distance: 1,000 feet.
   Direction: 68° from "s" in Anthonys Nose _____
4. Distance: 2,100 feet.
   Direction: 174° from "U" in PUTNAM _____
5. Distance: 2,200 feet.
   Direction: 24° from "r" in Sucker Brook _____

(The answers are found on page 225.)

Just for Fun Each player has a training map, a compass, paper and pencil, and a copy of the list given above. Players have ten minutes in which to finish the task. Correct answers score 20 points. The player with the highest score wins.

···

Compass Declination (or Variation)

As we explain compass declination to you, please take a deep breath and relax. Special orienteering maps feature blue lines indicating the declination of the map toward magnetic north. However, most maps do not, and it is a very important lesson, which at first can seem very complicated. But read along, and you'll find you've got it!

Let's continue our homework and remain on our imaginary hike. Let's assume that the training map is the actual map of the territory in which you want to hike, and that you are equipped with a protractor-type compass. The route you have just planned on pages 114–116 is the one you want to follow.

You arrive at your starting point at the crossroads south of Log Chapel. Open your map, and line up the side edge of the base plate of the compass to connect the starting point with the road-T north of Meadow Knoll Cemetery. Twist the compass housing to line up the orienting arrow with a north line on the map. Hold the compass with the direction-of-travel arrow pointing straight ahead of you, the north part of the compass needle pointing to the N of the compass housing. Line up a landmark in front of you. You are set to be on your way. Or are you?

You would be if *true north* of your map was the same as the *magnetic north* of your compass, and the geology of our continent did not affect the magnetized needle. But unfortunately, they are not the same, and geology does affect the needle.

The result is that true north and magnetic north are the same only along a line that runs off the west coast of Florida, through Lake Michigan, and on up to the Magnetic North Pole located north of Hudson Bay. On any location between this zero line and the Atlantic Ocean, the compass needle points west of the true-north line. On any location between the zero line and the Pacific Ocean, the compass needle points east of the true-north line. The angle between the direction the compass needle points and the true-north line is called the *declination*, or variation. It varies from 20 degrees west (20° W) in Maine to 30 degrees east (30° E) in parts of Alaska.

Locate your area on the maps on pages 120 and 121, and find the compass declination for your territory. Repeat it to yourself again and again until it is firmly established in your mind.

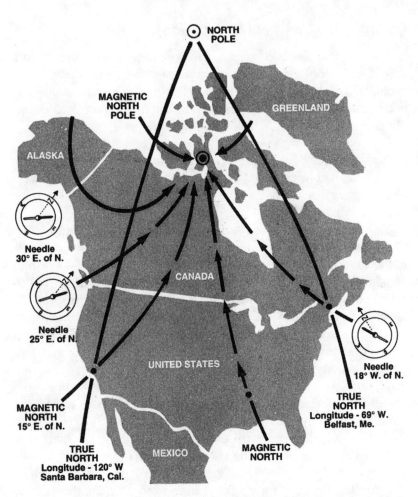

True north is the map direction toward the geographical North Pole. Magnetic north is the compass direction toward the Magnetic North Pole.

If you are traveling away from your home territory, check the compass declination in the bottom margin of the map you will be using (see page 40).

What Difference Does the Declination Make?

Why is it so important to know the declination of your location? Because you may be thrown completely off your intended course if you depend on a compass direction taken from a map without taking declination into consideration.

Let's use the example of a location where the declination is 15° W. Set your orienteering compass and blithely take off in the direction the direction-of-travel arrow points. Your course will be 15 degrees off! Whatever distance you travel, each degree off will result in an error one-sixtieth of the distance traveled. So, after you have traveled a distance of 3,000 feet, you will be *50 feet off for each degree of declination*. In this particular case, where the declination is 15 degrees, or 15 times 50 feet, that means you would be off by 750 feet. If you continue, *you will be one-quarter mile off after traveling only 1 mile*. No wonder you can't find your destination!

Fortunately, it is a simple matter on a modern orienteering compass to compensate for declination, so you will not be thrown off course. There are two ways to ensure your accuracy. You can reset the compass each time you set it from the map, or, even simpler, make your map speak "compass language." (*Note:* There are orienteering compasses with a declination setting device built in.)

Resetting your Compass for Declination

If your declination is west: Set your compass on your map in the usual way, lined up with the first leg of your route. Next, find your setting

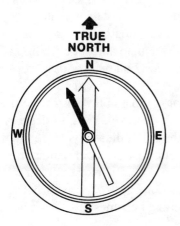

The magnetic force of Earth pulls the compass needle out of line with the true-north direction. The angle between the two directions is the declination.

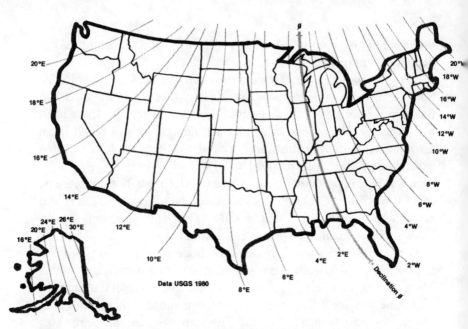

Declination chart of the United States, 1980. Magnetic north and true north coincide on a line west of Florida up through Lake Michigan. Other places have an easterly or westerly declination.

in degrees where the black index pointer under the rim indicates it to be. *Add* the number of degrees of the setting you read here. Twist the compass housing so that the index line is under the new number. The compass is now set for your map and your declination. Orienteers remember to add the degrees when the declination is west with the rhyme "Declination West, Compass Best," adding being a positive or best thing to do.

As an example, say you live where the declination is 9° W. You set your compass for a certain direction on the map and get a reading of 282°. You add 9 to 282 and get 291 degrees. You reset your compass to this new number (291°) and you are ready to proceed.

If your declination is east: Set your compass on your map in the usual way, lining up your first direction of travel. Find, in degrees, where the black index pointer under the rim indicates your bearing. *Subtract* the number of degrees of your easterly declination from the number of degrees of the setting you read here. Here you can remember the orienteers' rule "Declination East—Compass Least," since something subtracted from the setting becomes less than it was.

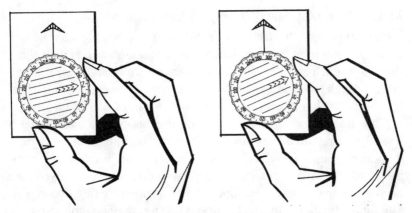

To compensate if declination is west: Check the number of degrees at the base of the direction line. Add the declination and reset your compass to the new number.

Twist the compass housing so that the index pointer is under the new number. The compass is now set for your map and your declination.

Let's take as an example if you live where the declination is 18°E. You set your compass for a certain direction on the map and get a reading of 144°. You subtract 18 from 144 and get 126. Reset your compass to this new number (126°), and go!

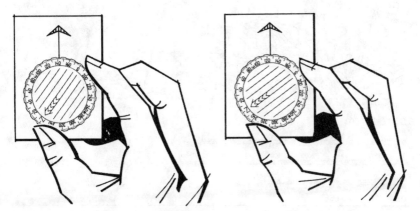

To compensate if declination is east: Check the number of degrees at the base of the direction line. Subtract the declination and reset your compass to the new number.

Making Your Map Speak "Compass Language"

Instead of going to the trouble of resetting the compass each time you take a bearing from the map, and possibly making an error each time, there is a much simpler way to compensate for declination. Having gone through the exercises above, however, will have given you a better understanding of declination and why we must consider it.

The simpler way involves providing the map with magnetic-north lines. By using these lines instead of the true-north lines of the regular meridians, your map will be speaking the same language as your compass, and you will have an easier time navigating. The settings you take on your compass using these lines do not require resetting to compensate for declination—the declination is taken care of automatically.

There are two ways of providing your map with these magnetic-north lines. The first is to use the map's magnetic-north line, and the second is to use the orienteering compass.

The simplest method is to draw a line, with great care, up through the map, in continuation of the magnetic-north half-arrow line in the bottom margin of the topographic map (in the right margin of the instructional training map in the back of this book.) Then carefully draw other lines parallel to this line, 1 or 2 inches apart (see illustration below). Take

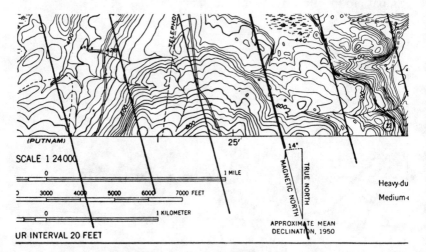

Make your map speak "compass language" by providing it with magnetic-north lines. The method shown here makes use of the map's declination diagram.

time off from your reading to draw such magnetic-north lines on your training map.

This method works well in most cases, but has some drawbacks.

Since the magnetic line on the diagram is very short, any straight-edge extension could result in considerable error. Also, in the cases of very small angles, the diagrams are sometimes exaggerated for the sake of clarity. So to be perfectly sure when using this method, first check the diagram angle between the magnetic-north half-arrow line and the true-north line to make certain that this angle is actually the number of degrees indicated.

The second, and more precise, method is to use an orienteering compass as a protractor.

For a map with a *westerly declination*, subtract the number of declination degrees from 360° (north), and set the compass dial at that number. If the declination is 14°, for example, you would set the dial at 346° (360° minus 14°). Now place the compass on the map. Align the north lines on the bottom of the transparent compass housing with the right border line of the map and draw your first magnetic-north line along the left edge of the base plate. Then add other parallel lines to it.

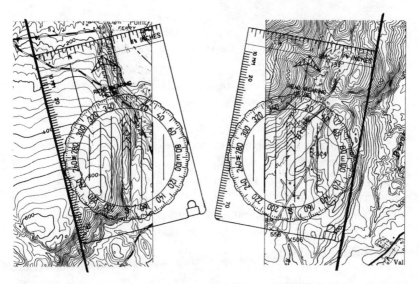

For a more precise way of making your map speak "compass language," set the orienteering compass for the declination and use the map border as a guide.

By using these magnetic-north lines whenever you take a bearing from the map, you can ignore the whole declination issue.

It can happen that the meridians, the true-north lines, on your map do not run parallel to the side margins. On your training map, they are parallel, which you can check by seeing that the longitude, 73° 22′30″, shown in the lower right corner is the same as in the upper right corner.

You can check this on a map that does not have the longitude indicated at the corners, but rather on the lower and upper margins. You have to draw a meridian from a longitude number in the lower margin of the map to the same number in the upper margin. If this line is parallel to the side margins, then you can use either the margins or this line for drawing your magnetic-north lines. If this line is off, then you have to draw your magnetic-north lines on the basis of the meridian line.

Traveling by Map and Compass: Orienteering

There are four basic instances for which you use your map and compass together:

1. To orient the map, using the compass
2. To transfer a bearing (direction) from the map to the compass, and then to the field
3. To transfer a field bearing set on the compass to the map
4. To measure distances on the map using the scales on the compass (see pages 47–48)

We will go over the first three in the pages that follow. After that, you should feel prepared for honest-to-goodness orienteering, or navigation, in the field. Start off with some short cross-country hikes through easy territory to practice your map and compass skills. If you live in a city, you can practice in one of the larger parks, provided you can get a detailed map of it. Such maps are available for many city parks, including Central Park in New York City.

Later on you can certainly plan longer trips through rougher terrain, and finally you will graduate into a full-fledged orienteer, whether you chose to try the sport of competitive orienteering, or whether you now have mastery of map and compass for personal use. You should soon be confident of your skills, even in true wilderness areas.

Getting Ready for Orienteering in the Field

For your first orienteering hike, get out the topographic map of your local area and plan a course to follow.

Choose an easily accessible starting point, pick four or five points in the terrain you would be interested in finding, and plan to end your trip back where you started. Take a friend the first time, or at least tell someone what you are up to for safety's sake, even if you are in a city park.

Orienting the Map with a Compass

Orienting a map, as you know from your course work (pages 53–54), means lining up the directions of the map with the same directions in the field. You can do it "by inspection," but it is an even simpler matter to orient using your orienteering compass.

There are two ways to do this.

1. **Using the Map's Declination Diagram** Set the orienteering compass at 360°. Then place it on the map so that the side edge of the base plate lies parallel with the magnetic-north line of the declination diagram in the margin of your map and with the direction-of-travel arrow toward north. Then turn the map with the compass lying on it until the north part of the compass needle points toward the N of the compass housing. The compass is now oriented—and so is the map.

2. **Using the Map's Magnetic-North Lines** Set the orienteering compass at 360°. Place it on the map so that the side edge of the base plate lies along one of the magnetic-north lines you have drawn on the map (as described on pages 124–125) and with the direction-of-travel arrow toward north. Then turn the map with the compass lying on it until the north part of the compass needle points to the N of the compass housing. The map is now oriented.

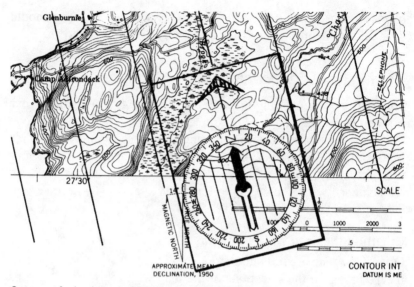

One way of orienting map with compass is to place the edge of the base plate parallel to the magnetic-north line, then turn the map until the compass on it is oriented.

Keep the Map Oriented While Reading It

At the start of an orienteering hike, you should orient the map to get a general idea of the lay of the land and of the route to follow. If you travel through terrain with only a few identifiable features and have to rely primarily on the compass for your directions, you won't have to repeatedly reorient the map. However, even if you are following your compass course, you should orient the map whenever you come to an object marked on the map, such as an open field, a swamp, a hill, a creek, or a trail. This procedure acts as a check to ensure your compass route is keeping you on the right track.

When you need new bearings for your travel, you can simply open up the map to the part containing the stretch of the route directly in front of you. You can fold the map up into a manageable size. Transfer the direction you want to follow from the map to your compass, so that the map and compass coincide as you move along.

The 1-2-3 Method to Transfer Bearings from Map to Field

Follow three simple steps: (1) Place your compass on the map; (2) set your compass by the map; and (3) set yourself by the compass.

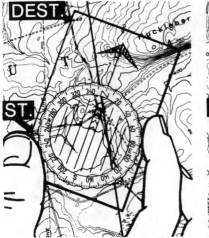

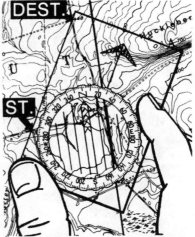

Step 1 in orienteering: On the map, line up the compass with the route from Start (ST.) to Destination (DEST.).

Step 2 in orienteering: On the compass, set the housing by aligning the orienting arrow with the magnetic-north line.

Step 1. On the map, line up your compass with your route. Place the orienteering compass on the map with the edge of its base plate touching both your starting point and your destination. Your direction-of-travel arrow must be pointing in the direction you want to go. Disregard the compass needle.

Step 2. On the compass, set the housing to the direction of your route. Hold the base plate firmly against the map with your left hand. With your right hand, turn the compass housing until the orienting arrow on the bottom of the housing lies parallel to the nearest magnetic-north line drawn on your map, with arrow point to the top. Disregard the compass needle. The compass is now set for the direction of your destination. By using the drawn-in magnetic-north line, you have automatically compensated for any compass declination in the area covered by your map.

Step 3. In the field, follow the direction set on the compass. Hold the compass level in front of you with the direction-of-travel arrow pointing straight ahead. Turn yourself by shifting your feet and moving your entire body while watching the compass needle

Step 3 in orienteering: In the field, follow the direction set on the compass. Hold the compass level in your hand. Turn yourself until the needle points to N on the housing. The direction-of-travel arrow now gives the direction to your destination.

With compass oriented, raise your eyes and pick a landmark in the direction in which the direction-of-travel arrow points. Walk to this landmark, then sight with the compass to the next landmark along your route. Continue to your destination.

until the needle lies directly over the orienting arrow on the bottom of the compass housing, with the north end of the needle pointing to N. The direction-of-travel arrow now points to your destination. Raise your head, and choose a landmark such as a rock, a large tree, or some other sighting point in that direction. Walk to that landmark without looking at your compass or your map. When you have reached it, again check the direction with your compass, on which you have been careful not to change the setting. Ahead is another landmark leading you closer to your destination.

When you have reached the first point of your "orienteering" hike (the destination you chose for your first leg), study your map again. Set the compass for the next leg. Continue until you have covered the whole route and are back at your starting point. You should feel a sense of accomplishment, having successfully negotiated your first orienteering expedition.

Transferring Field Bearings to the Map

You now know how to transfer a bearing from the map to the compass for a route you want to follow. Occasionally, though, you may need to reverse this action. You may need to transfer the bearings from the field to the map. For example, your compass can be used to identify on the map one or more visible, but distant, features from your known position. There are three steps to this process:

Step 1. Hold the compass in a level position in front of you, and using the direction-of-travel arrow, sight straight toward the object or bearing you'd like to transfer to the map. Next, turn only the compass housing until the N index is at the north end of the magnetic needle.

Step 2. Place the compass on the oriented map with the side of the base plate aligned from your known position. Turn the entire compass until the meridian lines of the housing are parallel to the magnetic-north lines of the map.

Step 3. Draw (or imagine extending) a line along the compass base plate and beyond in the direction you've sighted. This line should intersect known features on the map, making identification easy.

A similar procedure can be used to determine how far you've followed a course, as long as you can sight two landmarks that are identifiable on the map. Let's say you are not sure where you are on the map. In this case, you would follow Step 1 to determine the bearings toward each of the landmarks. For Step 2, though, align the compass base plate with each of the landmarks, one at a time. From both landmarks extend lines in the opposite direction of the bearings you took initially. The point where the two lines intersect is your current position, allowing you to see how far you have traveled along your course.

Try an Imaginary Orienteering "Hike"

After you have successfully completed some short-distance orienteering on your own or with a few friends, you'll want to try your newly acquired skills on a more ambitious scale. It's time to plan a course of about five miles through unfamiliar territory on the map, and then travel over that course in the field with map and compass.

To give you an idea of what you may experience on such a hike, open up the training map in the back of the book, decide on a number of points you want to hit, and try to figure out how you would proceed from point to point if you were actually out in that area. As an example, let's say you've picked the points shown on the maps on pages 136 and 137. You would start at the road-T north of Meadow Knoll Cemetery and wind up in the same spot after a clockwise trip to all the indicated points.

Clothing and Equipment

If this were a real hike in the great outdoors, you would need to consider what clothing and equipment you would want to have with you.

For comfort and safety during an orienteering hike, you will want to dress in comfortable old clothes suitable for the time of year and expected weather. Since you will possibly be crossing through underbrush (and maybe some poison ivy!), it is generally recommended to wear long pants, not shorts. Pay special attention to your socks, so that they don't bind or chafe or cause blisters. Consider your shoes carefully, as well, so you don't hobble into your last point. Most people these days will choose to wear sneakers, but for a hike, harder-soled shoes may be more appropriate. If you decide to get involved in competitive orienteering, there are other clothing recommendations we will make, but for now, be comfortable.

For equipment, you will need a topographic map of the territory you are exploring, your orienteering compass, a watch, and a pencil. In this day and age, you will probably have your cell phone, but turn off the ring tone (if you get service) so you can relax and enjoy nature! A whistle for emergencies is a lightweight security measure. You might want to bring along some lunch or a healthy snack, and some water.

Your Outdoor Manners

When you travel cross-country, you will probably at some point encounter areas where fire hazards exist, caused by drought, down timber, or dry leaves, grass, or weeds. A spark can set off a major forest fire. It is a self-imposed rule among orienteers never to smoke while on course. In fact, it is difficult these days to find orienteers who smoke at all.

Consideration of property is of prime importance in orienteering. Never trespass on private property. Usually, if you ask, permission will be given. Never walk over tilled or planted fields; always skirt the edge of the crop fields so as not to damage any growth. Always leave gates as you found them (opened or closed), and do your best not to disturb any farm animals. When it comes to public property, heed the directions of the park ranger and follow any printed regulations for the area.

Be Systematic: Steps in Orienteering

Properly clothed and equipped, and with the best resolutions in the world to remember your outdoors manners, you arrive at the spot you have designated as your starting point. As a beginner, you should also have told someone where you are going and when you intend to be back. You are eager to be on your way.

You never know who you'll meet when you are out exploring by map and compass... but be sure to mind your outdoor manners, including leaving any gates as you found them to keep from disturbing farm animals.

Not so fast.

For successful orienteering, there are certain practices that expert competitive orienteers and outdoorsmen have found of value. It is best you get in the habit right away of following a systematic checklist.

Step 1. Find your exact location on the map. For the imaginary hike, that would be easy. It would be at the road-T north of Meadow Knoll Cemetery.

Step 2. Find the exact location on the map of the point to which you are going and check the general direction to it. Study the map. The first point you want to hit is located at the crossroads a few hundred feet southeast of the "l" in Log Chapel. In map designation, that would be ¼ inch SE of the "l" in Log Chapel. There it is, about seven thousand feet to the west of your starting point.

Step 3. Draw in the beeline from the place where you are to the point where you want to be. Get out your pencil, then use the edge of the base plate of your compass to draw in this beeline.

Step 4. Decide on the most efficient route. Take a good look at your map. The beeline from your starting point to your first destination goes through a level stretch, then continues downhill, across a brook, up a cliff, then over more level ground. There are no specific landmarks on that line to help you determine whether you are on the right track or not. By changing your course slightly you will have plenty of help: you can cross a brook and follow a tributary almost the whole way to your destination (see maps on pages 136 and 137). And that is what you do.

Step 5. Set the compass correctly for cross-country traveling. Set the compass on the map from your starting point to the spot where the tributary runs into the book. What is the setting? 270°.

Step 6. Jot down the time you set out from one point to the next. Your map gives you the distance between the two points, and knowing the distance, you can figure out the approximate time it will take you to get to the next point. When that time is up, you should be close to your goal, and by watching your surroundings, you should have no trouble locating it.

Off You Go!

Having taken the steps described above, you are finally ready to go. Proceed on the route you have decided upon from starting point to point number 1of your orienteering course.

The first stretch is up over a cow pasture, with steep hills on either side of you. You reach the crest of the pasture and run down hill, through a grove of white cedars. At the bottom of the slope, you find the brook meandering along in slow motion.

You did not hit the T in the brook where the tributary comes in, but it should be nearby. Is it upstream or downstream? Study the map. The brook you intend to follow falls down over the cliff that is in front of you. You should be able to hear it. You listen. There it is—a bit upstream to your left. You climb the cliff right next to the gurgling

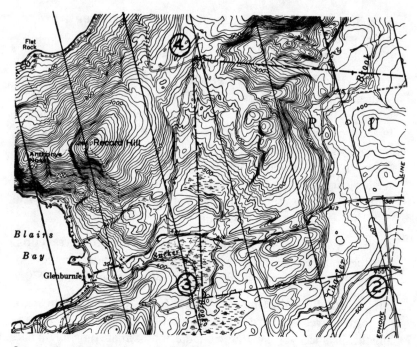

Open up the training map in the back of the book and locate the orienteering route shown on these two pages. You start at S (Start)...

water. It is a steep climb, but you make it and then the ground levels off, so it is easy. Be sure to follow along on the training map.

When you reach the dirt road where it bridges the brook, jog northwest of the road-T, then head west until you reach the crossroads south of Log Chapel. Keep checking your route on the training map.

You'll feel proud when you reach your first destination according to plan.

You are likely to feel some excitement now, as you're off to the next point—the crossroads ¾ of an inch on the map east of the "e" in the Charter Brook, about 2,800 feet in a west-northwesterly direction from where you are now.

Find the location on the map and lay out the beeline. This is an easy route. The beeline almost follows a road that goes directly to your second point. Just to be sure, check the direction of the road with your compass before you head off. You quickly reach the point

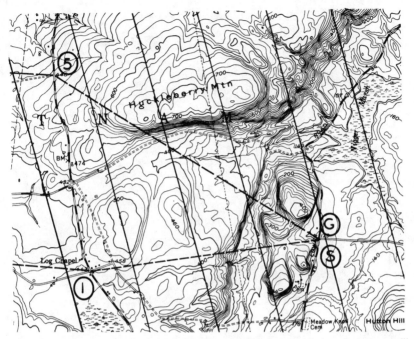

... proceed in a clockwise direction, and wind up at G (Goal). A description of what you will encounter en route is found on pages 135–140.

and prepare to proceed to point number 3—the road bend 1/16 of an inch north of the "B" in Sucker <u>B</u>rook. You have a fairly long stretch ahead of you—5,800 feet toward WSW.

For Speed, Use Roads

Draw the beeline on your map. It crosses the Charter Brook, then strikes some steep slopes, and skirts the tip of a swamp. Instead of following the straight line through that rough terrain, you realize it will be easier and faster to take the road southwestward toward the farmhouse. Cross Charter Brook now (the farmer probably has a footbridge you can use) and continue between two low hills and along the north edge of the swamp. Remember to follow along on your training map.

Follow the road to the first farmhouse on the right, get the farmer's permission to cross his land (since we are pretending,

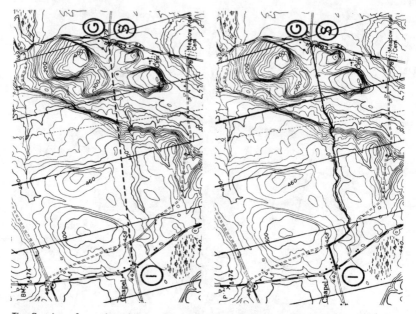

The first lap of your imaginary orienteering hike. Instead of taking a beeline, follow the brook, then roads, to the first destination.

we'll pretend you got permission), and use the bridge. Take a new bearing toward the road, leading between the two low hills, then just north of the swamp and to the road. In order to avoid the swamp, you had to take a bearing to the road north of the road bend you are looking for, so when you reach the road, turn south on it and find the spot. Here you study what to do about reaching point number 4. Point 4 is the road-Y 1½ inches NNE of the "l" in Record Hill—about 7,200 feet N of the spot where you are. The beeline to point 4 would be pretty tough: through a swamp, uphill, downhill, another swamp, then steeply uphill along a stream. So, very cleverly, you choose the roads instead, heading north until you reach your destination.

For general navigation for a hike, or for competitive orienteering, the challenge (and fun!) is in the variety of routes you can take to your goal. It is usually faster to try to find a road, so you can walk unencumbered by underbrush, rocky cliffs, slippery streams, or even knee-deep bogs. A road will let you jog or run and make some time, key to an orienteering race. However, you have to carefully judge which route to chose—and that's why orienteering is a sport for those who like to use their minds and bodies at the same time.

Cross-Country Phase

The next leg of your trip may be a real toughie—a mile and a half cross-country. Study the beeline you have penciled in on your training map. It may not be so hard, after all, if you head for the brook, follow it to the farmhouse, then proceed south on the road until you hit the footpath. Go east on the footpath and then on the unimproved road.

Set your compass for the farmhouse and start off. It is level at first but then goes downhill, with hemlock-covered slopes on both sides of you. Among a heap of boulders you find the bubbling spring that is the source of the brook. Make your way along the stream through a carpet of ferns, then along the grassy banks until you hit the farmhouse. Take a look out over the valley. This view would be worth returning to someday: there's even a beaver dam down by Charter Brook. Take a few minutes to enjoy the view, but keep on going, southward along the road, then eastward along the path.

Where is the path? Checking the training map, it should be right there at the road bend, but you can't see it. Fortunately, you are prepared for such a situation by having counted your steps from the farm. The location is right, but the path has been filled with a maze of undergrowth. You'll have to go by compass and hope to find the unimproved road that leads to point number 5.

Set your compass and continue. Sure enough, this is the path, because there is a footbridge across Charter Brook and a log across a tiny tributary. There's the unimproved road, and ahead is the road-T you are aiming for.

One more stretch to go—back to your starting point at the road-T 1¼ inches north of the "a" in Meadow Knoll Cemetery, about 9,500 feet SE.

There's Always Another Way

Locate your goal on the map. The beeline you drew earlier on the training map looks like it crosses some really rough terrain. It climbs up over part of Huckleberry Mountain, goes down a steep cliff, then continues up a steep hill and down the other side. There must be another, easier way to get there.

You decide to cut off a corner of Huckleberry Mountain and hit the unimproved dirt road south of it, then go east on the road until you hit the highway, and finally south on the highway to your goal.

You set your compass at 146° and continue on your journey.

It is fairly easy going now, over bare rocks in some spots, but from time to time you have to clamber among pine and huckleberry bushes and through brambles. You reach the dirt road—it is only a wagon rut but with a beautiful shady lane with overhanging branches. You have to be glad that you decided against climbing Huckleberry Mountain and sliding down its side. In fact, you pass a spot where you have a good view of the cliff, and there is a sheer drop of close to three hundred feet you couldn't possibly have crossed. The topographic map shows it, but now that you've seen it, you know you couldn't have gone that way.

You're nearly home; you don't even need to use your compass on this stretch. Look at the training map. It tells you where to go. You hit the main road just west of Niger Marsh and continue southward until you reach the road-T at the Meadow Knoll Cemetery.

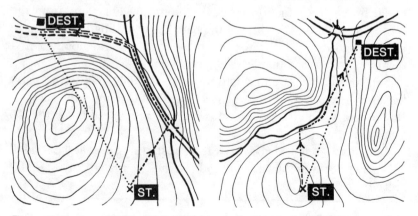

The good orienteer picks the most efficient route. (Left) Instead of climbing a mountain, aim for the bridge and follow the roads. (Right) Strike for a "collecting" landmark, such as a lakeshore, to get closer to your destination, then go by compass from there.

Now for the Real Thing

Your first orienteering hike has come to an end. Using your imagination, working with the training map and compass surely has given you a good idea of how interesting this can be. It's time to try the real thing. By now you know enough about the use of map and compass to enjoy a fairly ambitious undertaking. So, get going!

You will return home satisfied with yourself. You may have made a few mistakes en route, but that is the way to learn. With each orienteering hike, you'll get more comfortable and confident. It is very important to sit down after you get home and review your excursion by taking a second turn over the route, using only the map. One of the competitive orienteers' favorite pastimes is exchanging experiences and tips after they finish the course. Right now, you'll learn a lot by rehashing the choices you made by yourself or with family and friends.

Plan more and more orienteering trips. The outdoors awaits to challenge you and your new skills.

Orienteering will become more than a new skill. It will become your way to locate hidden fishing streams off the beaten track, to undertake more ambitious hunting expeditions, to vacation by canoe in some beautiful wilderness area, or to take your family on an adventuresome picnic.

As you'll see, orienteering is interesting and enjoyable, but it is not necessarily an end in itself. You'll get practice and more practice in the proper and intelligent use of map and compass for finding your way in unknown territory anywhere in the world.

Setting Out

Once all preparations and precautions have been taken care of, it's time to set out. If your qualifications are as good as they should be for the trip you have planned, you should be able to carry it out with flying colors, and have the time of your life.

But there is that little *if*. If you are not completely positive about your qualifications for an expedition on your own, always take a more experienced friend, or even a registered guide. You can even tell him or her that you want to learn by doing as much as possible on your own. Eventually you'll have the necessary training and confidence needed.

In any event, as we have said before, even for shorter hikes, tell someone where you planning to go. You won't be able to charge your cell phone out there if you plan to be gone several days or more. If the area you are exploring has a forest ranger or a game warden, tell them where you are going. The unforeseen can happen, no matter how well prepared you are. You want help to be able to find you if you need it.

Know Where You Are

As you travel along, the most important rule is to know at all times where you are, according to your map; and know the direction in which you are going, according to your compass. Some people like to use a GPS as an aid, but remember its limitations!

Before you set out from one point to the next, determine your exact position on the map. Then orient your map, and follow map and compass bearings to your next destination. Figure out the distance and the approximate time it should take you to get there. When using the compass, follow the bearing carefully from landmark to landmark. Check your progress by identifying land features in the terrain with those on the map whenever possible as you travel. You will soon develop a sense of where you are at all times—based upon constantly checking your map, compass, and landmarks—that will follow you even as you navigate your "regular" day-to-day environment.

When in Doubt . . .

In spite of all your orienteering skills, there may be times when you feel in doubt about your location or direction. What can you do?

There is one thing you cannot do. You cannot get lost with a map and compass in your hands—if you use your brain. So, stop and think. Take a few deep breaths. Do not panic! With a bit of figuring and logical reasoning, you should get back on course.

First of all—did you set your compass bearing correctly from your map? Did you compensate for declination by using a map provided with magnetic-north lines that automatically take care of the declination? If you did, your destination will probably still be ahead of you. Your progress could have been slower than you expected. If you did not compensate for the declination, your destination may be waiting to one side of you—to the right of you in areas of westerly declination; to the left in areas of easterly declination.

If you still find yourself stymied, you may decide to return to the last location of which you are positive by following the back-reading of your compass. To do this, travel backward against the direction-of-travel arrow instead of with it, as described on page 84. Even better, if there is a long collecting landmark ahead of you, such as a road, a river, or a lakeshore that you can use to guide you, aim for that and then reschedule your trip from there. You can also look for landmarks in the distance beyond your goal, called catching landmarks (such as easily recognizable mountain tops), to tell you if you've gone too far, or use cross-bearings to find your location (see pages 104–106).

Most important is to avoid any possibility of going wrong by following all you have learned about the practices of correct orienteering. Plan your trip carefully before you start. Use a map provided with magnetic-north lines. Set your compass correctly for each stretch of your journey. Refer to your map repeatedly to know where you are. Follow your compass and trust it to get you to your destination.

Practice makes perfect, they say, and this is certainly true in orienteering. The more practice you get, the more confident you become, and the less apt you are to ever be in doubt of your location on your trips.

Enjoy shorter, family treks. Try some competitive orienteering, or at least use a local orienteering club to test your skills. Gradually, you may want to add an overnight trip, and eventually even something as ambitious as a weeklong wilderness trip. With enough practice and preparation, you'll be safe and have great fun exploring the magnificent nature on this great planet.

Hints on Wilderness Orienteering

If you are an ambitious lover of the outdoors, you may eventually want to use your orienteering skills for extensive travel through wilderness areas. Such treks are certainly not for beginners. There are many related skills that must be mastered before you can undertake something as challenging as a week or a month in unfamiliar wilderness territory. Take as many shorter day excursions as you can fit in. As we've suggested before, join a local orienteering club. Even if competitive orienteering isn't for you, you will gain lots of experience among more veteran enthusiasts, who will be willing to help you along. Getting involved with the Boy and Girl Scouts is an excellent source of great practice, as are other local groups that you can find on the Internet or through a local outdoor equipment store.

Training for Wilderness Travel

In addition to the ability to use a map and compass accurately, there are other important skills you will need to master before you set out on a wilderness journey. There are many books and Web sites on general hiking and camping skills, and others devoted to wilderness hiking and orienteering. Reading can help, but of course, these skills can only be mastered with real practice in the field. To get confidence and control, you need to get out there.

Hiking Skills For a short hike near home, you don't need any special equipment or any special training. Covering an extended route is a different story. You must know what footgear and clothing to use and bring as spares. You have to know how to walk with the least amount of excess effort, and when and how to rest. Safety and first aid are very important, in case of an accident far from medical services.

Backpacking Skills When your trip calls for spending several nights in the open, you must know how to take care of yourself: what equipment to pick and how to carry it; what food you need, and how to transport and prepare it; what campsite to choose; how to pitch a tent and prepare a camp; how to build and extinguish a fire; what sanitary arrangements are necessary; and how to leave a campsite.

Canoeing Skills If you expect to do all or any of your traveling by canoe, a lot of specialized training is necessary before you set out. This can be a fun and memorable way to travel, but you need to be a very good swimmer and completely at ease in the water. Of course, you need to know how to handle a canoe, how to launch and land it, what strokes to use under various conditions, how to prepare the canoe for portage and the actual technique of portage—essentially, how to be safe on lakes and rivers under all possible weather conditions.

Planning Your Extended Trip

The first thing you will have to decide is where you want to go. Study the map of the United States and Canada, or anywhere in the world, and there will be plenty of wonderful places to choose from—national parks, national forests, wilderness areas, state parks, provincial parks, and more are scattered all over. For canoeing, you would obviously want to choose an area with wilderness lakes and waterways, such as Maine, Minnesota, New York, and Wisconsin, or New Brunswick, Ontario, and Quebec.

You'll need to secure topographic maps of the areas you want to explore. With the Internet, it is very easy to find many suitable sources. The United States Geological Survey at www.topomaps .usgs.gov is, of course, a great source for U.S. maps. As technology advances, there are ways to download maps to your computer, to your phone, and to your Global Positioning System. That is fine, but we recommend you always have a real copy of the topographical map in your possession. Have a plastic folder or plastic wrap to keep it dry. If all your electronic devices fail you, you will still have your trusty map and compass.

State and county park maps can be picked up or ordered from state and county visitors' bureaus and Chambers of Commerce. Again, the Internet is a huge asset in finding what you are looking for. Most states will have special information for travelers, campers, hunters, and fishermen.

Laying Out Your Route

Lay out the route you intend to follow, through what you think will be a suitable area. Don't be overambitious. A daily stint of ten or so miles of hiking, or around fifteen miles of canoeing, is probably all you will want to do, even if you are in good condition. Don't plan

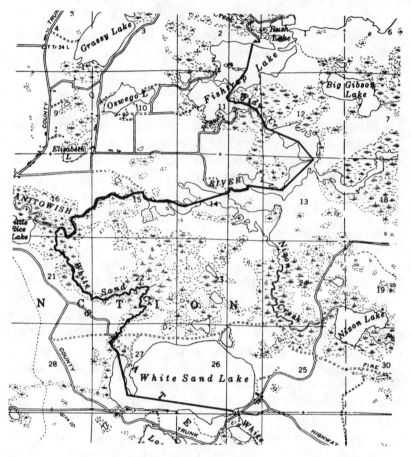

Lay out your tentative canoe route on a topographic map, then secure local information. Straight lines indicate routes traveled by compass.

on being on the trail every day of your expedition. Schedule certain days for stopovers where you can enjoy your outdoor hobbies, such as hunting or fishing, photography, nature study, or just relaxing.

Getting Local Information

When you have decided on your route, be sure to secure as much local information as you can. Again, the Internet has made this so easy, but you can contact the visitors' bureau, Chamber of Commerce, or

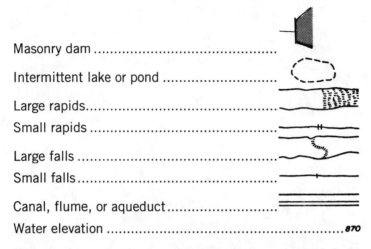

Masonry dam ....

Intermittent lake or pond ....

Large rapids..

Small rapids ....

Large falls ....

Small falls...

Canal, flume, or aqueduct............................

Water elevation *870*

When planning a canoe trip, pay special attention to these map symbols. Rapids are for the trained canoeist only; falls necessitate portaging.

even the local Post Office or general store, by mailing a self-addressed return envelope. Remember that printed materials you have found can be out of date.

Even if you don't have your own computer, it is so easy these days to go to a local library to find all the information you might want. You can get weather updates and predictions. Before you go, you need to know where equipment can be bought or rented, whether food supplies can be purchased along the route or if they need to be toted, what campsites are available, and what the regulations are for their use. If you are canoeing, you will also want to know whether certain streams are navigable and which portages are passable.

Understanding and having confidence in your map and compass skills truly opens up the world to you. Enjoy.

PART 4

CHALLENGE
Competitive Orienteering

The last control point looked interesting on the map—a deserted tenant farmer's cottage named Outward Glimpse. It looked easy to find—a good thing, considering I'd experienced some problems earlier in the competitive orienteering event. I wanted to make up as much time as possible because team selection for the next weekend's relay championship was only a day away.

I decided that the fastest, safest route was to follow a trail south to a point where I could see a small lake on the left, then take an exact bearing with my new protractor-plate compass toward the cottage.

Following my route as planned, I veered off the trail when the lake came into view and headed on a direct bearing toward the cottage. Once in the dense forest, I heard some breaking branches both to my left and to my right. Good, I thought, there were still other people on the course. It should take me no more than fifteen minutes to get to the cottage, if my estimation of distance on the map was correct.

Anticipating that the farmer's cottage would be located in a small clearing, I expected the woods to thin out and brighten as I approached the control point. Soon I stumbled across an old fence. It was partly fallen, surrounding an abandoned outpost of humanity just beyond. The scene was one of the most moving I'd ever encountered in my travels through the woods during orienteering competitions. It wasn't awe-inspiring like a wide-angle canyon vista, nor was it so compressed by the young, growing forest that breezes couldn't penetrate.

In the gleaming sun of the still frosty spring morning, I saw the control flag. It was hanging against the northern wall of an old barn shaken by decades of winds and weather. Shafts of sunlight squirted through cracks and holes in its wallboards, slicing through the darkened interior like swords. In a beautiful old apple tree partly covered with moss that resembled an old man's beard, a thrush sang aloud the joy and pleasure of the clean, quiet morning air. Nothing else remained of the cottage but a fieldstone foundation.

In the air around this former home, I sensed the farmers' painstaking work, their young wives' tender affection and morning diligence in caring for their families. Their hard times seemed drowned out by the songs of the birds in the apple tree.

But some of their despair sunk straight to the heart of this rambling orienteer. It stuck in my throat as I contemplated the insignificant remains of these hard-working pioneers. In time, what will there be left here on Earth of all of our efforts, our successes and failures, our work and play, our love and hatred?

Possibly nothing more than disintegrating boards in a barn for the sun and winds to play through, or a profound silence celebrated in the songs of the birds in the trees.

Competitive orienteers don't often have the time to notice the tracks of our forefathers in the woods. But the sense of history here was so strong—in the air, in the rustling branches of the trees, in the singing of the birds—I couldn't ignore it.

I felt like I had experienced a divine service. I left the spot with tears in my eyes, but enriched in my soul. I couldn't linger to ponder how quickly things change, how short our time is on Earth, how amazing life is, because I heard another runner approaching the control from behind. I'd like to think he felt the depth of the moment like I had, but we couldn't look each other in the eyes.

—**Björn Kjellström**

The History of the Sport of Orienteering

The competitive sport of orienteering can be defined as a timed cross-country race, covering unfamiliar territory, using a map and compass to find markers, or "control points," on a course. Originating in Northern Europe, competitive orienteering has developed into a very high-tech sport that attracts millions of participants. The largest event in the world is the annual O-ringen in Sweden, which in 2009 had some 8,000 racers from forty-three countries—not spectators, but active participants! Add in the families, spectators, officials, volunteers, and media and over 24,000 people took part!

Military land navigation training events had been held off and on in Scandinavia since the late 1800s. Orienteering as a competitive sport appears to have gotten its start at a race organized in 1919 outside of Stockholm. A group of Swedish youth leaders were encouraged by an enthusiastic sportsman, Major Ernst Killander, to give this former military activity a serious try as a competitive sport for the general public.

In the 1920s, the sport developed slowly. In the early 1930s, a new type of compass, the Silva Protractor compass, gave the sport of orienteering a real boost, because it made the learning of map and compass use easier. This new style compass was manufactured and marketed by inventors Gunnar Tillander and brothers Björn and Alvar Kjellström, successful orienteering champions themselves. They went on, with

Björn Kjellström as president of Silva, to become the leading manufacturers of compasses worldwide for decades. (Björn Kjellström, of course, also became the author of this book.)

After the war years in the 1940s, the sport of orienteering started to spread all over the world. It is popular in Europe, Japan, Australia, and New Zealand and is becoming increasingly well known in North America. There are movements to get orienteering into the Olympics, and World Championships are fiercely competitive. (Go to www.orienteering.org for more information from the International Orienteering Federation.) The World Championships in orienteering were held in the United States for the first time in 1993 at West Point, New York.

The international growth of the sport has contributed to the development of high-quality, large-scale detailed maps just for orienteering. Those first racers in Scandinavia used black and white 1:100,000 scale maps issued by the government. Today, the International Orienteering Federation, with close to fifty member nations, sets the rules for and supervises its World Championship and World Cup Series. It also has set standards for highly detailed orienteering maps, which are becoming easier to find. Orienteering maps are full-color, with a scale of 1:15,000 or 1:10,000, making even large boulders identifiable. Special lines help with the declination issue, with lines going to magnetic north featured in blue.

One of the greatest aspects of the sport of orienteering is that just about anyone can participate. At local competitions, you are really competing against yourself to improve your skills. National and international meets have become very serious challenges among highly trained athletes, using modern, high-technology equipment.

Orienteering has fostered true international fellowships, with serious orienteers taking their vacations abroad where they can participate in three-, four-, or five-day affairs, sleeping in campers or tents or with families in the host countries. The O-ringen event in Sweden, with some 25,000 competitors and followers, features many races at many levels, and the camping area becomes a small city of orienteering enthusiasts. It is not unusual for orienteers from "more advanced orienteering countries" to volunteer with instruction, coaching, and map-drawing in areas where competitive orienteering is still getting a foothold.

Leaders in outdoor education have found that different types of competitive orienteering create greater interest in learning how to use a map and compass, and therefore in all phases of outdoor life. As a result, orienteering events are becoming more numerous at schools and various clubs. Orienteering events have also become popular in the scouting world, arranged by Scout councils and by individual Scout and Explorer units. Eagle Scouts have helped build permanent orienteering courses in local parks.

The word "race" for these types of outdoor events is somewhat of a misnomer. It isn't speed alone that determines the winner in orienteering, but a combination of the following:

1. Correct interpretation of instructions
2. Careful planning of routes to be followed
3. Intelligent use of map and compass
4. Time used to cover the entire course

Orienteering is called a "thinking sport," in which mental ability supports and often outweighs physical ability. It may be described, as an Australian orienteer has suggested, as "cunning running," where the cunning is generally more important than the running.

An especially fast runner may get off to a poor start by failing to follow instructions or by not studying the map carefully enough when deciding on the best possible route. He may be careless in making compass settings or orienting the map and compass before racing off.

To win an orienteering race, it pays for each participant to start out easy, to spend sufficient time in checking and rechecking, and to figure out the most advantageous way to proceed, for his or her particular physical ability. Over the mountain, or around it? This is especially true for the beginner. By the time you have caught the orienteering bug and have become proficient in the sport, your speed across country will have improved with your skill in using the map and compass.

Orienteering as a Sport

An orienteering race can be included in any kind of outdoor activity. It can be a special all-day event staged at any time of the year for a group of young people or adults or be open to the public.

It can be the theme for a day at any camp or Scout troop meeting. Some athletic clubs use orienteering as part of their physical fitness programs. For any group interested in map and compass work, from military units to search-and-rescue groups, there is no better way than combining your field work with orienteering: it is the best way of learning navigation while building self-confidence.

An orienteering race can be an easy activity for untrained or unskilled people of all ages or it can be developed into a highly competitive event among experts, whether they are individuals or teams. An orienteering club specifically dedicated to the sport of orienteering can schedule a string of races of different lengths and varying difficulty for training its members and interested individuals in the intricacies and strategies of the sport.

Whether it's a local, national, or international event, certain requirements must be met for a successful orienteering challenge:

Suitable Terrain The area presented should preferably be undulating and well-wooded with several readily identifiable natural or man-made features.

Maps A topographic map or preferably a map especially prepared for competitive orienteering should be available for each person or team.

Compasses An orienteering compass should be available for each person or team (usually participants will own their own compass, but there should be some available for newcomers).

Markers A marker locating each control point should be placed along the course. The international standard is three-sided nylon. Each side has white on top and orange on the bottom, divided diagonally from top right to bottom left. For introductory sessions, you can fashion your own controls, using empty boxes, pieces of wood, or even paper plates; painting them the proper colors would add to the scene.

Personnel You need plenty of cheerful volunteers to be course setters, starters, timers, and other helpers. As you move from casual practice races to serious competitive events, other officials should be on hand.

Waivers Please check whether your group needs insurance or a waiver for people to sign to release you from any legal obligation, should someone get hurt. Unfortunately, in this day and age, this is something you have to ask about. Groups like the Boy Scouts and 4H usually have coverage, and many public parks will assist you in getting what you need.

Types of Competitive Orienteering

Competitive orienteering has evolved to where the International Orienteering Federation recognizes four kinds of orienteering: foot orienteering, mountain bike orienteering, ski orienteering, and trail orienteering. Go to their Web site to learn more (www.orienteering .org).

Generally speaking, there are two main types of competitive orienteering, though people are having great fun adding variations.

1. **Cross-Country or Point-to-Point Orienteering** In what is considered the more traditional approach, the course setter chooses controls in the field for the participants to find, but individual participants must determine their own routes from one known control to the next.
2. **Preset-Course Orienteering** The course setter not only picks controls in the field for the participants to find, but also chooses and presets the route the participants must follow from one unknown control to the next throughout the entire course.

Variations of Point-to-Point Orienteering

The most important feature of point-to-point orienteering is the opportunities it gives the orienteer to make quick decisions and sound choices of routes, based on full knowledge of the proper use of map and compass.

Of the several possible variations of this type, cross-country orienteering is by far the most popular and traditional. It is what most people think of when they hear the term "orienteering" and is also called "foot orienteering."

Two variations—score and relay orienteering, both involving the free choice of routes—have also attained great popularity. The main reason for this is that, while cross-country orienteering is a personal battle of quickness of mind and physical stamina of each participant against all the others, score and relay orienteering permit team participation of small or even fairly large groups working together.

Cross-Country Orienteering
Race

Outdoor Project

Objective Test of mental quickness in choosing the best possible routes between controls and of mental agility and physical stamina in following these routes efficiently using map and compass.

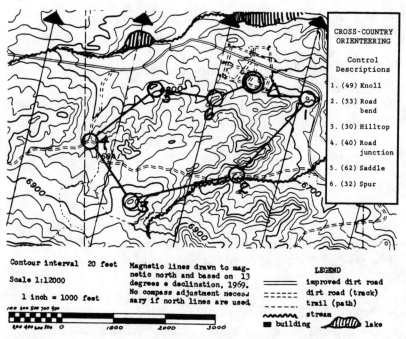

CROSS-COUNTRY
ORIENTEERING

Control
Descriptions

1. (49) Knoll

2. (53) Road
        bend

3. (30) Hilltop

4. (40) Road
        junction

5. (62) Saddle

6. (32) Spur

Contour interval 20 feet

Scale 1:12000

1 inch = 1000 feet

Magnetic lines drawn to magnetic north and based on 13 degrees e declination, 1969. No compass adjustment necessary if north lines are used.

LEGEND

========= improved dirt road

------- dirt road (track)

------- trail (path)

~~~~~~ stream

■ building ▨▨▨▨ lake

In cross-country orienteering, each participant determines the routes to follow to reach the control points marked on a master map.

Group Activity The predetermined course setter chooses several readily identifiable natural or man-made features on suitable terrain from a map of the area. For juniors and beginners, the course setter selects five to twelve of these features of different degrees of difficulty at varying distances apart (300 to 1,500 feet, or 100 to 500 meters), forming a more or less circular route 1½ to 2½ miles (2.5 to 4 kilometers) long. For elite orienteers, the courses are usually 8 to 10 miles (12 to 16 kilometers) long.

The course setter visits each control in the field, determines its exact location on a master map, and proceeds to develop a course. When determining the order in which the controls should be visited, the course setter makes it more interesting and challenging by choosing controls that offer several route choices. Before the race, the course setter places an orange and white orienteering marker at the exact location of each control, as indicated on the master map.

The participants are provided with a map of the area and a control description list, giving a brief description of where the control is, such as "road bend" or "boulder cluster." The International Orienteering Federation has standardized the maps and symbols used so that language barriers are eliminated. The full set of IOF Control Descriptions can be found at www.orienteering.org. You will want to learn them, or print them out, when you start going to more formal meets organized by official orienteering clubs. They are the standardized way to describe control features in international orienteering, designed to prevent language barriers among orienteers from different countries. Beginners will usually be given symbols and a short word description. The racers are started at one- or two-minute intervals, with their start time duly noted.

For some events, especially the bigger ones, the control points are actually printed on the maps. At smaller, local meets, the participants go from the start area to a master map, where they very carefully copy the controls and course from the displayed master map onto their own map. They then decide their course to the first control, taking bearings as learned, on the routes they have chosen for themselves.

Whenever a racer reaches a control, he or she secures proof of having found it by marking the proper space on their cards with the code symbol or with the attached control punch. The race is won by the participant who hits all of the controls in the prescribed order, and arrives at the finish in the shortest amount of time.

Objective To test the participants' ability to plan effectively a series of routes, comparing time involved, and a test of orienteering skills in general.

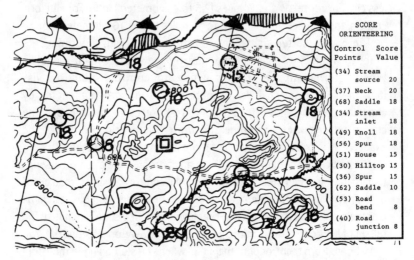

SCORE ORIENTEERING	
Control Points	Score Value
(34) Stream source	20
(37) Neck	20
(68) Saddle	18
(34) Stream inlet	18
(49) Knoll	18
(56) Spur	18
(51) House	15
(30) Hilltop	15
(36) Spur	15
(62) Saddle	10
(53) Road bend	8
(40) Road junction	8

In score orienteering, each participant strives to earn as many score points as possible by hitting the controls that have the highest value.

Group Activity Score orienteering differs from cross-country orienteering by the fact that the controls are *not* to be visited in any specified sequence. Instead, each control is given a certain score value, or number of points. Controls farthest away or hardest to find are given the most points, say 30 to 50 points each. The easier or closer ones may be valued at 5 to 15 points.

The course setter goes about the task exactly as for cross-country orienteering, selecting the control locations and plotting them on a master map. But instead of selecting controls to be arranged into a course to be visited in a specific sequence, the course setter picks control locations to be visited at random within a radius of 1 mile from the combined start-and-finish area (covering about three square miles). The course setter picks so many locations that no one could visit them all in the given time limit of, say, ninety minutes. The course setter assigns point values to each control, gives each control a number, and prepares a description list of the controls with their number and score value ("behind the knoll by the swamp, number 6, 20 points").

Individual Competition Before the actual start, each participant is provided with a map of the area and a description list of the controls with their point values indicated. Sometimes, the course will be preprinted on the map. If not, participants proceed to the master map area, where they use an allotted time period, often fifteen minutes, to copy the control locations onto their own maps, to decide how many controls to try to visit and the order in which they will visit them. The participants are started.

The objective is now for each racer to score the highest number of points within the time limit. This is done by locating as many control points as possible and marking the control card with the coded punch at each point as proof of having reached them. If the time limit is exceeded, the participant is penalized by having a certain number of points subtracted from the score. The penalty is usually 1 or 2 points per minute overtime. A participant arriving at the finish five minutes late would thus have 5 or 10 points subtracted from the score. Note that there is no incentive for taking less than the allotted time to finish. If you are fast, you are better off trying to get to another marker, but not if that attempt will cause you to use too much time! It is a great way to learn to judge time needed, as well as a way to perfect your map and compass skills. The race is won by the person who has the highest score after subtracting possible penalty points.

Team Competition Score orienteering adapts itself very well to team competition, one of the reasons it has become so popular. Team events can be handled in different ways.

> **First method** Each team member works independently. He or she decides individually what controls to reach, what routes to set, and how to run them, as described above. At the conclusion, after all team members have arrived at the finish, the score may be decided (a) by totaling the scores of all team members and dividing by the number of members to come up with an average score, or (b) by totaling the scores of the three highest-scoring participants, if the team consists of three, four, or five members, or of the five highest scores if the team has five, six, seven, or eight members.

> **Second method** A team captain distributes all the control locations among team members. He or she may decide to use strategy, sending the best orienteers to the farthest and hardest control locations, and the beginners to the closest and easiest spots. When everyone has

returned, the score points of all the controls reached are added up and any time penalties are subtracted to figure the team total.

··

Relay Orienteering   Outdoor Project
·····································   ···

Objective To use orienteering for team building or establishing team spirit within a club or a group, and to further train individual members in the skills of orienteering; it is the most popular team competition in orienteering.

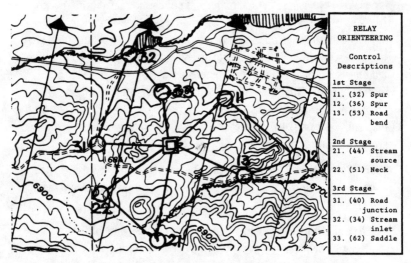

RELAY ORIENTEERING

Control Descriptions

1st Stage
11. (32) Spur
12. (36) Spur
13. (53) Road bend

2nd Stage
21. (44) Stream source
22. (51) Neck

3rd Stage
31. (40) Road junction
32. (34) Stream inlet
33. (62) Saddle

Relay orienteering is a team competition in which the team members fan out from a central point (double square) to cover several short courses.

Group Activity Relay orienteering is cross-country orienteering turned into a team event. As in all other kinds of orienteering, the course setter begins by choosing suitable terrain that is appropriately mapped. Next, he or she decides on a central, combined start-changeover-finish area and on a number of control points. The location and arrangement of these controls will depend on the number of members of each team. If there are three members to a team, the course may consist of three stages fanning out from the central area in the form of a clover leaf, with each member running a leaflet, consisting of two or three controls. If there are four members, a butterfly course can be creatively set, with each team member running one of the four wings. With five to eight members, a star course can be set. (For more elaborate relay competition, start and finish can be separated and more changeover stations can be added so you can use your creativity to set the course.) The controls are set up and the master maps developed in the same way as for cross-country orienteering.

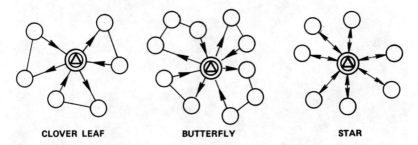

| CLOVER LEAF | BUTTERFLY | STAR |

The course for relay orienteering can assume varying shapes, depending on the number of orienteers to be accommodated.

At the start of the race, the first participant from each team is given a map and a control description sheet, then started off. The time is taken for the team. Participants run to the master map area and copy the locations of the controls they are to find onto their own maps.

They take off to reach their controls and to secure proof of having visited them by marking the team's control card with the code symbol or punch card. When they have completed their stage, they turn the control card and map over to the next racers, who then run their stages. When the last runner finishes for each team, time is taken and the score for the whole team is calculated. The race is won by the team that hits all its assigned controls and arrives at the finish in the shortest amount of time.

Wayfaring, or Map Hiking

Outdoor Project

Objective To give noncompetitive persons a chance to enjoy the outdoors and the sport of orienteering at their leisure.

Group Activity At an orienteering event, the organizers may open up the easiest course or a special course for young and old who like hiking but who are not particularly interested in the competitive aspects of orienteering or who aren't confident enough in their abilities as orienteers.

Wayfaring, or map hiking, is a great way for people to go at their own pace, yet add challenge to their hike by following an orienteering course.

This simple form of orienteering is particularly suited for families with young children. It provides an extra challenge beyond the general demands of hiking and gives a feeling of accomplishment as they hit the controls along the course.

Participants entering into this leisurely kind of map hiking—wayfaring—are provided with a master map of the territory with course and control points indicated. They take off to follow the course at their own speed, stopping to enjoy the landscape and beauty of nature whenever they feel like it. They can also combine their hike with bird or plant study or other investigation of nature. Some may want to go on to try competitive orienteering or may choose to continue going at a slower pace.

Preset-Course Orienteering

Preset-course orienteering is a more leisurely type than point-to-point. It is often used as a training event.

The two main variations of this type—line orienteering and route orienteering—supplement each other. In line orienteering, participants follow a route indicated by a continuous line on the master map. In route orienteering, the participants mark on their maps the location of the controls they find along a trail marked with streamers.

Preset-course orienteering can also be used to test various skills not related directly to the use of map and compass, as in ski orienteering.

Line Orienteering   Outdoor Project

Objective To test the ability to follow a route indicated on a master map with map and compass.

Group Activity The course setter proceeds in exactly the same way as for a cross-country orienteering event, choosing a suitable terrain and selecting

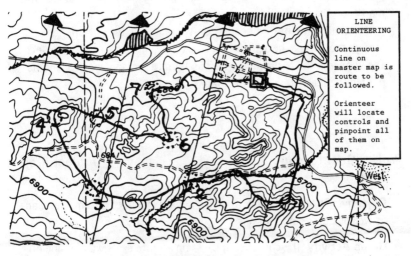

LINE
ORIENTEERING

Continuous line on master map is route to be followed.

Orienteer will locate controls and pinpoint all of them on map.

In line orienteering, each participant follows a course drawn on a master map. In route orienteering, participants draw the controls on their own maps.

five to twelve control points. The course should be more or less circular with a combined start-finish and a length of about 2 to 4 miles. The course setter visits each control, determines its exact location on the map, and puts a numbered control marker on it. From this step on, however, the picture changes: instead of marking the control locations on the master map, the course setter presets the course to be followed by drawing on the map the exact route he or she desires the participants to follow from one control to another. Some of the legs that must be followed may be along paths, roads, streams, and lakeshores that can be followed by map alone. Others may be cross-country legs on direct bearings through woods and over fields that can be followed only by compass.

At the starting point, the participants are provided with maps of the area and then started off at intervals to the master map area. The intervals need to be rather long to prevent one racer from stepping on the heels of the one in front of him, possibly three, four or five minutes, depending on the number of participants. At the master map area, the participants copy onto their own maps the route to be followed, then take off to follow it by map and compass. If the route is followed correctly, the participants will pass all the control points in numerical order. Their task is now to plot on their own map exactly where the control point is found, by circling the place on their map in pen or pencil and noting the code symbol of the marker on the score card.

Normally, time has no bearing on winning this type of orienteering, though there has to be a predetermined time limit announced in advance. The winner is the participant who has found the most controls and has plotted them accurately on the map.

Project Orienteering
Outdoor Project

Objective To test the ability to follow a route indicated on a master map, as well as other outdoor skills.

Group Activity The course setter sets up a route exactly as for line orienteering. On the day of the event, each control is staffed with a project official who informs the participants of the project to be performed and how their performance will be scored. Such projects may be related to orienteering: Landmark Hunt (pages 61–62), for example, or Finding Bearings (pages 81–82). Or the projects can be unrelated, though testing outdoor skills, scouting information, or nature identification is a great idea. Some challenges might be: "make a fire with two matches," "collect a single leaf from each of ten different kinds of trees," or "identify five different bird species."

The participants may work as individuals, as buddies, or in small groups, such as a Scout patrol. They proceed as for line orienteering, performing the different projects at each control. The winner is the participant or team that has the highest total score for the various projects, including a score for a map with correctly plotted controls.

Route Orienteering   Outdoor Project

Objective To test the ability to plot on a map the location of controls the participants pass when they follow a trail marked with streamers.

Group Activity The course setter prepares for the event basically the same way as for cross-country orienteering and line orienteering. Route orienteering is ideal for beginners, since it is impossible to get lost! The distance should be kept to between 1 and 3 miles. When the course setter has established the course, he or she follows it and marks it by tying colored streamers—plastic or cloth, so they don't rip and litter—to trees, fence posts, and other objects. The streamers should be set so that the next one can always be seen along the trail. The course should preferably follow things that are identifiable on the map: trails, creek beds, ridges, or other clear landmarks. The control markers are usually set every 800 to 1,200 feet.

At the starting point, the participants are provided with maps of the area and started off at one- or two-minute intervals to follow the clearly marked course. The task of the participants is to follow the course on the map at all times, so they know exactly where they are. When they come to a control marker, they circle the location on the map as precisely as possible.

The winner will be the participant who turns in the map with the most correctly marked controls. Any mistakes cause a deduction of, for example, 2 points for every sixteenth of an inch of error from a total of 100 points for all controls accurately marked. Time taken for the route may also be counted as a factor in deciding the winner, if you want. If so, the penalty for incorrectly marked controls could add two minutes to the score for every sixteenth of an inch of error.

The participants can also be asked to draw the entire course taken, the route as well as the control points, as they follow it. If two or more participants end with the same points, the winner will be the one with the most correctly drawn route.

***

Ski Orienteering   Outdoor Project

Objective Can be to make cross-country skiing more interesting by combining skiing with the skills of orienteering, but is also a serious international-level sport, governed by the International Orienteering Federation. At the top levels, it is a grueling endurance sport, where the athlete uses his excellent skiing and map reading skills to make hundreds of route selections for the fastest way to each control. For the purpose of this book, we will discuss a lower-level, local event.

Group Activity The course setter proceeds with the preparation in the same way as for that type of foot orienteering chosen for the event. The most simple ski orienteering events to organize are line orienteering and route orienteering, as there are no special preparations needed. But to organize cross-country orienteering on skis, certain preparations may be necessary.

A suitable terrain for cross-country ski orienteering is quite different from that needed for foot orienteering. For the skiing competition, you will need an area with many tracks and trails. The course setter may have to add more tracks and trails, using a snowmobile or a team of skiers. All tracks and trails, even those freshly made for the purpose, will have to be marked on all of the maps. Depending on the terrain, the snow conditions, and the skiing ability of the participants, the course may be from 3 to 10 miles long. The control points should be few and easy to locate for the skier who arrives in the vicinity. The basis of the competition should be the route choice, not a frantic final search for the control marker.

Controls should be located at fixed and clearly visible features of the landscape on or fairly close to the tracks.

At the starting point, the participants are provided with maps of the area with the course and control points already marked. They are started at two- or three-minute intervals. As in foot orienteering, the task of each participant is to follow the course, locate the controls, and return within a certain time limit.

The winner is the participant who has located all the controls and has returned to the finish line in the shortest time. A participant who misses a control may be penalized a period of time or can be disqualified. Those who have located all the controls should be placed ahead of those who had penalty points for missed controls. Time should be a secondary factor in the case of ties.

Mountain Bike Orienteering — Outdoor Project

Objective To add challenge to mountain biking by demanding skills such as quick-thinking route choice and map memory. Expert bike handling is a must, as is the strength for up- and down-hill tracks. To protect the environment, bikes are usually required to stay on existing paths. It started in the late 1980s at club level in countries where mountain biking was a popular outdoor sport. World Championships in mountain bike orienteering are now governed every year by the International Orienteering Federation. In 2009, orienteers from twenty-three countries participated in the World Championships in New Zealand, as mountain bike orienteering continues to grow in popularity.

Group Activity Setting up the course for mountain bike orienteering is not unlike that for ski orienteering. Remember, if you are practicing on your own or setting up an informal practice with friends, have fun but respect the environment of the area.

Trail Orienteering | **Outdoor Project**

Objective To open the joys and challenges of the sport of orienteering to everyone, including people with limited mobility. Manual or power wheelchairs are permitted, as are canes, crutches, and other mobility aids, since speed is not part of the competition. The International Orienteering Federation governs international Trail-O classes, including an annual World Championship.

Trail orienteering is a version of competitive orienteering that allows people with limited mobility to compete using wheelchairs and other assistive devices.

Group Activity The course setter chooses a route along wheelchair-accessible terrain and marks it appropriately. Clusters of control markers are set up. Competitors are given very detailed maps with control descriptions. The challenge is to decide which, if any, of the controls relate to the feature on their map. Both able-bodied participants and those with disabilities must locate control points from a distance. The markers are usually identified as A through E, from left to right, when marked on the special control card. Cards may be marked by an escort. An easy electronic system is being tested in some areas. Because the goal is accuracy and no racing or route choice is involved, people with physical limitations can compete on equal terms.

....

ROGAINE Orienteering ⟨✦⟩ Outdoor Project

Objective To dramatically increase the challenges of score orienteering for those who just can't get enough! ROGAINE stands for "rugged outdoor groups activity involving navigation and endurance." Twelve to twenty-four hours in duration, a ROGAINE event tests participating teams' abilities to properly plan long-distance wilderness travels, while confronting a variety of physical and mental challenges. Night orienteering, with the additional difficulties it presents, creates a heightened level of excitement and challenges for experienced teams.

Group Activity For safety reasons, ROGAINE orienteering should be attempted only by teams of two to five people who know one another's roles and abilities. Cooperation and coordination are crucial, since teams are not allowed to split up. The objective is simple: using only a map and compass, and traveling by foot, to visit as many check-off points as possible during the predetermined time.

Each check-off point is assigned a specific number of points. Total points earned by the end of the event, minus any penalty points for finishing over the time allowed, determine the finishing order of teams.

A ROGAINE course setter establishes a start and finish (which may be in the same place) and sets up a sufficient number of check-off points over a large area to prevent teams from visiting all of them in the allotted time. Because of the long duration of a ROGAINE event, a designated central base camp provides food and a place to rest for competitors.

The increasing popularity of ROGAINE orienteering is due to its emphasis on fitness, teamwork, and the enjoyment of the outdoors. Even beginners are welcomed at ROGAINE events, since organizers usually try to set easier courses closer to the base camp, allowing novice teams the opportunity to explore and practice orienteering skills at a less challenging pace. Volunteering is also a good way to get a feel for what is expected.

Short-Distance Orienteering

Outdoor Project

Objective To test a participant's ability to speedily navigate a short course that has been set to require frequent decision making and concentration.

Group Activity Participation in short-distance events, also known as Short-O, is for individuals, not teams. Because speed is essential, competitors must overcome fast-developing physical and mental challenges. The winner must visit all designated check-off points and finish the course in the least amount of time.

Course setters must consider the following objectives: use terrain suited for running, establish check-off points in a location and sequence that demand frequent navigation decisions, and keep courses short enough to allow completion in about thirty minutes.

Short-distance events can use either mass, group starts or individual, interval starts. To prevent people from just following one another without navigating, the courses can be carefully set to route individuals on different overlapping loops before bringing them together for the final loop and an exciting sprint to the finish.

Orienteering on horseback! Why not?

Other Varieties

Almost all of the orienteering variations can be run with different means of travel. There are events for canoeists, horseback riders, and even city dwellers (perhaps on skateboards?). Other varieties are limited only by your imagination.

Your First Orienteering Race

After you have practiced on your own or with friends for a while, you will come to feel so competent in the skills of using map and compass that you have gained from this book that you will want to test your ability in competition with others interested in the sport of orienteering. Start by going online or contacting the United States Orienteering Federation to find a club in your area. Since orienteering is still growing in this country, you may have to travel a ways to get to a club. But contact them, get on their mailing list, and soon you'll find a meet to attend.

The newsletter or Web site for the club will tell you about various meets and if there are different-level courses for beginners, novices, and advanced being offered. You will get basic information such as date, time, location, and other details. Ask beforehand if you have any questions.

An ambitious, well-run, and established orienteering club might offer many courses, as in the example below.

Courses

Streamer	1.3 km	No climb	4 controls	Free course for kids with orange streamers marking the path
White	2.9 km	65 m climb	8 controls	Beginner course: many linear features, including streams and trails
Yellow	3.3 km	72 m climb	10 controls	Advanced beginner course: easily identifiable relocation features
Orange	3.5 km	92 m climb	10 controls	Intermediate course: check-off points on major terrain features
Brown	4.1 km	132 m climb	10 controls	Expert course: navigation is very tricky with few relocation features
Green	5.2 km	162 m climb	10 controls	Expert course: navigation is very tricky with few relocation features
Red	7.3 km	255 m climb	14 controls	Expert course: navigation is very tricky with few relocation features
Blue	9.4 km	315 m climb	20 controls	Expert course: navigation is very tricky with few relocation features

Bring an orienteering compass, a red ballpoint pen to mark the map, a plastic bag or folder to protect your map, a wristwatch, water to drink, and some lunch or snack.

Clothing for your first race does not have to be the fancy, slick expert orienteer's suit. Long pants and a long-sleeved shirt are recommended to help you avoid the likes of brambles, poison ivy, and ticks. Light hiking shoes are nice, but sneakers are fine for now. You will probably get them wet and muddy, but wait until you are really serious before you order those snazzy, cleated orienteering shoes.

You might try volunteering at an orienteering meet. You will be very much appreciated, will learn a lot, and will meet a lot of great people, eager to share their love of the sport.

Procedure

The day of your big event, be sure to leave home early. You can't miss registration! You'll be parking next to the other cars, some of them with out-of-state plates. Walk over to the assembly area, where lots of orienteers are already waiting, some in special orienteering suits, some with O-club shirts, some in hiking clothes, like you.

The information about the event will have given you a time frame for registration, so go over to the table and sign up! You'll be given a control card with your name and start time on it. You may be asked to pay a small fee for the map. You may have to sign a limited liability waiver. At some events, you will be given a "bib" with a number on it to help keep track of participants. You will also be told what time you must come back and sign in by, even if you haven't finished the course. For safety reasons, you must let people know you are back, so they don't send out the search-and-rescue teams while you're actually comfortably home in your bathtub!

Starting areas can be set up in different ways. A recorder and timer's table will be there. Report in to the recorder, and the timer will send each runner off at the time they have been designated. There may be three call-up lines, and you will be told where to go. Or there may be a starting grid, which can look like a 9-foot-by-9-foot grid with 3-foot squares inside. When it is your turn, you take your place behind two racers in your line. This last box is sometimes called the "get in" box. When the whistle blows, the runners in the front row take off.

```
        NONESUCH ORIENTEERING CLUB

Cross-Country Orienteering, September 15

        Description Sheet for
              WHITE COURSE
         6 controls, 3.1 km

1. (49)  KNOLL      4. (40)  ROAD JUNCTION

2. (53)  ROAD BEND  5. (62)  SADDLE

3. (30)  HILLTOP    6. (32)  SPUR

     Safety bearing: 360° (North)
```

For a small, local competition, a simple description of the control locations will suffice. As you get more sophisticated, official IOF cards and symbols should be used.

The people in the subsequent boxes move forward, and new racers step into the "get in" box. The people next to you will probably have control cards in their hands for different courses than yours.

You are now in the second box, also called the "get ready" box. Here you likely will be presented with a slip of paper with your course description. The official will usually remind you that the controls must be visited in the order given and that you must punch the proper square of your control card with the pin punch or clipper found on the control (the top races now use electronic timers and punch systems, but you probably won't see them at the local level). This proves that you have been there, but also gives you a way to check that you have found the correct control, since there are numbers you can match.

How often the whistle blows depends on how many runners there are, the length of the course, and how far apart the organizers are trying to keep the racers. It can be as frequent as every minute.

When the whistle blows and the group in front of you takes off, you are in the final "get set" position. Here you are usually given the map of the area of your course. (See illustration on page 156.) You won't have much time, but a quick look at our example shows the map has a scale of 1 inch to 1,000 feet and contour intervals of 20 feet. Our example also has the magnetic north-south lines drawn

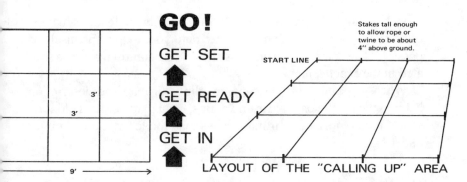

GO!

GET SET

GET READY

GET IN

Stakes tall enough to allow rope or twine to be about 4″ above ground.

START LINE

3′

3′

9′

LAYOUT OF THE "CALLING UP" AREA

A popular layout for the calling-up area consists of a 9-foot square divided with ropes into 3-foot squares in which the orienteers take their places.

in, so you won't have to go through that process. The fellow next to you in our imaginary race suggests you tip off each magnetic north arrow with a red arrow so there will be no question where north is on your map.

Finally, the whistle blast you have been waiting for is sounded: "Go!"

The Master Maps

Many orienteering races now use maps with preprinted courses. But the use of a master map from which you must copy your course is still common. The master map area at some races is positioned before the start. There is usually a big crowd of people craning their necks to accurately draw the locations of the controls they need to find on their maps.

In our example, the master maps are found after the start, mounted on pieces of plywood. It is nice if participants are started with enough time in between to have only one person at the map at one time. You can't take too long, but you have to be sure to copy accurately or you will really have trouble finishing the course. The area where you are now standing with the maps is indicated by a triangle. Each control point you are to visit is circled (about 5 millimeters in diameter) in purple or red. The circles are numbered and connected in numerical order by straight lines. (See page 156.) Your immediate job is to copy the circles, the numbers, and the lines onto your map as precisely as possible. The center of the circle is critical: the control marker is situated in the exact center.

When you have finished copying, slip your map and description list into the plastic bag, clear folder, or special map holder. Fold it up so not much more of your map shows than the leg you are about to undertake.

The Race

You are ready to run the first leg in our imaginary race—from the master map area to control 1, (49) Knoll. This should be easy. It is a short distance on fairly level ground, close and parallel to a road.

You first orient your map as this book has shown you. Familiarize yourself with the map and terrain.

Take a quick look around, then set your orienteering compass for the bearing and take off. You see the road to your left almost all the time. It helps give you confidence, so you can use a comfortably brisk pace (don't get worn out this early!). You see the bright orange and white marker from about 50 feet away. When you reach it, you check the number with the one on your control card. It is indeed number 49, as shown on your control description, so you use the special punch that dangles from the marker to punch your card in the right spot.

Now, for control 2, (53) Road Bend. Study the map. This could be a toughie. The direct beeline would take you up and over a hill of seven contour intervals, 140 feet. Remember what you've learned from your practice sessions: there's always another way. Studying the map, you realize there is an improved road a short distance to the east. Follow it south until you hit the dirt road, then continue west until you arrive at control 2. Check the number on the marker and punch or stamp your card in the correct box.

To get from control 2 to control 3, (30) Hilltop, you wonder whether you should continue along the road, then strike out at the appropriate spot. But there are no clear landmarks to determine where to get off the road. So you set your compass and take off on the bearing up an incline, then across a fairly flat plateau covered with pines and fallen

The exciting start of an orienteering race: At the signal, the orienteers in the front line of the starting grid take off.

Racers in master-map area transferring control points to their own maps.

After deciding on a route, young and old race off for the first control.

The control point has been reached. Now the control card is marked.

A quick check with compass on map, and it is off to the next control!

The finish of a national orienteering event: the orienteers race full speed along the marked route to the finish line, applauded by the spectators.

trees here and there. You find the control, check the number, and punch your card.

From control 3 to control 4, (40) Road Junction, you notice that the beeline would take you down one contour interval and up another. Which route might be better for you? You quickly decide that the easiest route is southwest on the contour to the trail, then along the trail westward first, then northward to the junction. That's the route you follow, and you easily find control 4. Remember not to be distracted by other racers. They may be in another division, and this control marker may be on both courses!

You decide to take controls 5, (62) Saddle, and 6, (32) Spur, on straight compass, because the terrain looks relatively easy to cross. You reach them without any special difficulty, except for having to run through some stretches of undergrowth that cut down your speed.

Finish Procedure

At control 6, you have reached the last control of the "white" course. The race is almost over. Now you just have to cross the finish line. The route back from the last control is marked with colored streamers, so jog along the marked trail at a pace you can maintain until you see the finish banner. Then pick up your speed to arrive in the style of a real orienteer, as fast as you can muster. You did it!

Turn in your control card. An official will write your finish time on it and figure out the time elapsed. You've beaten the three-hour time limit. Another official checks the punch marks on your control card: the six spaces are marked correctly and in the right order.

You mingle with the other orienteers who have finished their courses. It is always great fun to compare adventures you had en route. People enjoy telling each other how they made out and have fun comparing the way they hit the different control points. Someone will have gone through the swamp and almost lost a shoe, while someone else might have been running so fast on the trail to make time that they missed the landmark they had chosen for cutting in to find the control.

After a while, the results are posted. No, you weren't the winner this time out, but you weren't the last one in, either. You feel very satisfied with your first orienteering competition and will probably do it again. Join the club!

Hints on Competitive Orienteering

As you get better and better at competitive orienteering, you will try harder and harder courses and maybe some of the variations we talked about earlier. You will soon see that competitive orienteering at its top levels is a serious endurance and thinking sport, where constantly evolving technology plays a role. Elite orienteering involves electronic timers and control cards, mapping and course-setting software, and race organizing software, not to mention specially designed clothing and shoes. As in any sport, if you get serious, you can spend money! If you do get really serious, you may want to attend some workshops around the country, and you may want to pick up some books that specifically deal with the top levels of the sport. Check out specific rules at www.orienteering.org. You'll also be working on your fitness, and an easy, energy-saving running style.

But even as an enthusiastic novice, you'll find it is worth becoming familiar with some of the most common techniques for effectively choosing the routes between controls and in following those routes with greatest precision.

Choosing Your Routes

Choosing your route starts while you are still copying the control locations and beelines between them from the master map onto your own map. As you do so, you get a general mental picture of the course as a whole and of the landscape through which you will be traveling.

You begin to formulate the quickest and least exhausting route from one control to the next, one that with certainty will lead you to the next marker. The choice of the right route may determine whether you win or lose the race. Before making a blind stab at arriving at your route choice, ask yourself:

- From what direction should I attack the control?
- What landmarks can I use to guide me?
- What obstacles will be in my way?

Attack Points

An attack point in orienteering is a large, recognizable feature clearly shown on the map and reasonably easy to find. It could be a road crossing, a stream junction, a bridge, or a large boulder. Since controls are very rarely placed on prominent features of the landscape, using attack points can be a useful strategy.

A clever course setter will probably choose control points that can only be reached by precision orienteering. The easiest way to decide from which side to approach a given control can be to go backward: study the immediate vicinity of the control for a prominent landscape feature that can be fairly easily reached and clearly identified.

After selecting a feasible attack point, study the map for all feasible ways to get to it. Decide whether to use the beeline drawn on your map or whether to go to the left or right of it. Once you reach your landmark attack point, use precision orienteering to find your control.

Guidance in the Field

There are usually a great number of special features shown on your map that will assist you in your route choice to find your attack point or control marker.

Handrails A handrail in orienteering terminology is a long, linear feature that runs more or less parallel to the direction in which you are supposed to go. Using one, if you can, is a good strategy because you can confidently travel along at a good pace, knowing you are headed the right way.

A road or path is, of course, the most obvious handrail. A power or telephone line can work well, as can fences or railroads. Man-made landmarks tend to be straighter.

A handrail is a long feature that runs more or less parallel to the direction in which you are supposed to go.

Handrails can also be natural features, such as a stream, the edge of a field or a clearing, a ridge, or a valley. A fast-moving stream may be easier to follow than a slow one, which might meander along in winding curves. As you get more skilled, more subtle lines on the map can be used as handrails.

Your least obvious handrail, but one of the most helpful ones, is the sun. Don't overlook it as a most valuable direction pointer once you have your direction established. In open terrain, you can use the sun in your face; with the sun behind you, you can follow your own shadow. Even at a side angle, the sun can give you assistance in retaining your set direction. In wooded areas with occasional open spaces, you can use the shadows cast by the trees in the same fashion.

Keep in mind, of course, that the position of the sun is always changing, and you will have to make adjustments, especially over longer distances. You will probably find that you'll use this handrail a lot outside of orienteering, now that you have become so much more aware of where you are all the time.

Check-off points To be on the safe side, the route you finally decide on should have a reasonable number of natural check-off points that will assure you that you are on the right course. Such points should be conspicuous features that are clearly marked on your map. You can make a mental note as you pass these landmarks of where exactly you are on your map as you near your control. Moving your thumb along your route on your map as you pass them is a good way to keep track of where you are.

The same kind of feature that will make a good attack point at the end of your route will make a good check-off point along the route. For example, the cliff should be on your right for part of your route, the pond should be ahead on the left, the bend in the road where you are to leave to run cross-country, the spot where the power line crosses the road, and many more.

You will also want to consider what orienteers call "collecting features," landmarks that lie between you and your control that help verify you are headed in the right way. The term "catching feature" is used for landmarks that lie beyond the control that warn you that you have gone too far.

Overcoming Obstacles

In choosing your route from one control point to the next, you will find that the straight line is not always the best for saving time and energy. As a matter of fact, the course setter will have seen to it that you have some obstacles in your way that will force you to make a choice of routes. Such obstacles may be hills or valleys, forests or bogs, lakes or marshes, cliffs or quarries. You will quickly need to make up your mind whether to tackle the obstacle straight on or to choose a route around it, whether to pick a route that is short but tough or longer but easier. It's all up to you, and no two paths taken will be exactly the same.

Over or Around? There is nothing quite so tiring and time-consuming as climbing a hill or a mountain, as opposed to running on level ground. So before climbing, check the elevation of the obstacle in front of you and decide if it would be better to go around. Of course, make sure going around doesn't take you through a quick sand trap!

Expert orienteers have reached the conclusion that for every contour interval of 20 feet they have to climb—the vertical distance of each interval on your 1:24,000 map—they expend the time and energy equivalent to running 250 feet on level ground, in addition to the direct horizontal distance shown on the map.

Let's say that on the leg to your next control, you run up against a hill that rises 80 feet—four contour intervals—with a horizontal distance of 300 feet. Using the formula above, you arrive at four times 250 feet, plus 300 feet—a total of 1,300 feet. Obviously, a detour less than that distance, say, 1,000 feet, should work to your advantage, provided that you will have no difficulty locating the next control on the other side of the hill.

If you are a good runner but only a fair climber, you might want to take the detour contouring around the hill—that is, keeping yourself at the same contour elevation. If you are a good climber, you would go straight up and over. Most expert orienteers would probably make the climb unless the face of the hill or mountain was exceptionally steep or the route around was not much longer. It's always a matter of choice!

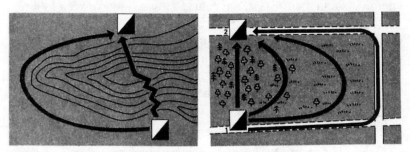

When you meet an obstacle such as a hill, you must decide whether to go over or around. If the obstacle is a forest, the question is, "Through or around?"

Through or Around? It isn't just elevation you need to think about in making your route choice. The vegetation you encounter also needs to be considered. Should you be faced with dense forest or areas covered with brambles or tall grass, or a semi-open forest with light undergrowth, you may want to study your map for the possibility that roads and trails surrounding the area may bring you more quickly to your destination.

So, during your training for competitive orienteering, you may want to find out how long it takes you to cover a certain distance—say, a thousand feet—along roads and paths and through various kinds of vegetation. Your results may look something like this:

Terrain	Time to cover 1,000 feet	Ratio	Distance covered in 2 minutes
Roads and paths	2 minutes	1	1,000 feet
Tall grass	4 minutes	2	500 feet
Forest with light underbrush	6 minutes	3	333 feet
Dense forest or bramble area	8 minutes	4	250 feet

By comparing the time needed for running through dense forest toward your destination with the time it will take you to reach it by roads and paths, you will see that for each 250 feet through dense forest, you will be better off on roads and paths as long as the distance is less than four times as long, or less than 1,000 feet. Similarly, you will shave one third off your time and energy by running along grassland rather than through a forest with light undergrowth.

Definitely Around Obstacles you must definitely go around are ponds and lakes, swamps and bogs, newly planted crops and cultivated fields, and outcrops and restricted areas (private property).

If you can see across an obstacle, simply pick a prominent feature on the other side—a large tree, a boulder, a house—in the compass direction toward the next control. Then run around the obstacle until you hit the landmark and follow the bearing still set on your compass.

If the obstacle is large and clearly marked on your map, such as a lake, you might get around it by striking out for one end of it and then taking a new direct bearing from the end point of the obstacle toward your control point.

Finalizing the Route

With a suitable attack point considered and with full awareness of all guidance and obstacles ahead of you, you can now decide on the route you want to follow. For quick reference, you may want to indicate it on your map with a thin line of your red ballpoint pen.

Make up your mind to stick to the route in a general way, but be flexible enough to make whatever changes may be necessary to solve special problems you may encounter.

Following Your Routes

Once you have decided on the route to the next control, you are off!

You can compare what you are about to do to teeing off in golf. First, you give the ball a bold whack in the direction of the tee in the direction of the next fairway. Then, you take smaller, more careful shots to get it onto the green and as close to the hole as possible. Finally, the precise putt will send the ball into the hole.

An even better analogy is the "traffic light" principle adopted by most elite orienteers. The idea here is the same as driving a car. If a green light is ahead, you drive on at full, safe speed. Yellow tells you to slow down and proceed with care. At red, you roll up to the line and come to a halt. Using this principle in orienteering, you will judge the difficulty of the different segments ahead of you. Grade them into segments of green, yellow, and red and proceed accordingly.

Rough Orienteering (Green Light) This would be for the first part of the leg that takes you from your present location toward a collecting feature or along a handrail in the direction of the next control or check-off point along route. To cover this stretch, you will use what is called "rough orienteering" and run at full speed.

Standard Orienteering (Yellow Light) You have reached the collecting feature and now have to locate the attack point that will bring you close to your next control. You keep a fairly good speed and go in for standard orienteering techniques by map and compass, keeping track of the distance traveled.

Precision Orienteering (Red Light) The final part of the leg, from attack point to control, requires precision orienteering: exact map reading, precision setting and following of compass, and accurate measuring of distance on map with accurate pace counting to match.

Under some conditions, you may have to switch temporarily from rough to standard or precision orienteering and vice versa in your travel and navigation between control points. Normally, though, you'll go from rough to standard to precision—and there is the control!

Rough Orienteering (Green Light)

Rough orienteering is for our green light phase, moving quickly toward a collecting feature or to an easy-to-find check-off point. It involves rough map reading and rough compass setting and following.

Set the compass on the map for the bearing to the next control or to the attack point you intend to use. Before taking the compass off the map, orient the map, pointing the line for the route to be followed in the correct direction. Finally, orient yourself, facing the direction you are to go.

Rough Compass Hold the compass at waist height in the usual way and turn your entire body around until the compass is oriented, with the north part of the needle lying directly over the north-pointing arrow of the compass housing. Your compass is ready to act as your steering instrument, guiding you along a straight route in the field.

Raise your eyes and look far ahead for a prominent "steering mark" in the exact direction in which the direction-of-travel arrow points such as a distant hilltop, a church spire, or a radio tower. Then run at full speed toward the steering mark. Beyond the first steering mark, aim for another landmark in the direction you want to go. Continue running, checking your compass only once in a while, and even then slowing down only long enough for the needle to come to a rest. You may have planned your route to a handrail along the way. In that case, shift your attention from the compass to the handrail and proceed toward the attack point.

Whenever you reach a check-off point, stop long enough to orient your map and to check whether to continue on the planned route or to reconsider. Then reset the compass on the map for the next bearing. When you become an expert orienteer, you may not even place the compass on the map for doing the job; you simply judge the next bearing by comparing the route line with the magnetic north-south lines on the map, twist the compass housing to the appropriate number of degrees, orient yourself in the compass direction, and run the next stretch.

Rough Map Reading While running on the compass, check the map from time to time to make certain that the landscape picture in front of you coincides with what you see on the map and to make sure that you reach the check-off points along the route. For example, are the cliff that is supposed to be on your right and the lake to the left actually there and being passed according to plan? So that you will know at all times exactly where you are, keep the map oriented by inspection and, as needed, by compass, letting your thumb follow the route along the map.

Keeping your map oriented necessitates that you shift its position in your hand each time you change direction along the route. If your direction is north, all printing will read right side up. If you are running south, the printing will be upside down. If you are headed east or west, you should be holding the map to line up with the direction you are going. Get into the habit of always keeping the map oriented when you read it, holding the map so that you easily can follow along. You can ignore the printing, since the names and other text have little importance when you are out in the field.

For rough map reading, do not bother with details. Get a general idea of the landscape, with emphasis on prominent features. Follow the route you have decided on, changing it only to overcome obstacles or situations that might arise.

Aiming Off Controls are often placed in the vicinity of a spot where a collecting feature is met or crossed by another feature. A control may be placed, for example, close to where a small stream runs into a larger one or where a path joins a road. In such cases, the actual juncture would be a logical attack point. To locate the juncture, however, you need to know at what point to hit the collecting feature so that you will not be running toward the right when you should be going left or vice versa.

To assure this, make use of an orienteering technique known as "aiming off." In this strategy, instead of aiming directly at the exact location of the juncture, you aim off your compass by setting it toward a point 100 to 200 feet (30 to 60 meters) to the right or left of the juncture, depending on its character and the distance to it. The longer the distance, the more you aim off to be safe.

When using joining streams as a collecting feature, aim slightly upstream. When you hit the stream, you will know that you have to run downstream to find the river junction near which the control is located. In the case of joining roads, you can aim to the left or to the right as you prefer. It is usually easier to find the larger collecting feature first and then use it to find the control.

In aiming off toward a stream juncture, aim off upstream and follow the stream downstream to the juncture (left). Aim off left or right for a road juncture (right).

Standard Orienteering (Yellow Light)

After running full speed through the green light segment of your route, you reach a point where you realize that more care is needed. An imaginary yellow light is flashing and demands that you make more exact use of the orienteering skills you have developed. It is a matter of locating and passing all of the check-off points you have on your map that lead you in the right direction.

Standard Map and Compass Reading From the very beginning, you have been running with your map oriented so that you had a general idea of the landscape in front of you. Now you need to follow your progress from check-off point to check-off point with greater care.

Fold your map so the immediate part of the leg you are running will show. Place your thumb on the map with your nail pointing in the direction you want to go. Keep your nail edge precisely over the spot where you are now standing. As you proceed, check every point you pass on the route and move your thumb so that its place on the map is always where you are. This method, "map reading by thumb," is the most effective kind of map reading. It permits sharper analysis of the terrain ahead and reduces the risk for error.

To save time, some orienteers combine map reading by thumb with the process of using the compass. After the compass has been set for the proper bearing, they carry the compass and the map in the same hand, holding them firmly together with the edge of the compass lined up with the route on the map and the direction-of-travel arrow pointing forward. They then keep compass, map, and themselves oriented by always keeping the north part of the compass needle over the north arrow of the compass housing. With this arrangement, the front right-hand or left-hand corner of the base plate takes the place of the thumb, turning map reading by thumb into map reading by compass corner. As you proceed, slide the compass over the map, always keeping the corner at your location. When the route changes direction, simply shift the compass and reset the housing to the magnetic lines. It takes some practice, but you'll get it!

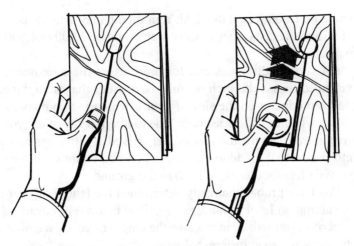

Orienteers use map reading by thumb to follow their progress on the map. For even more exactness you can use the map reading by compass corner method.

With the compass set, follow the bearing in the usual way, by aiming for steering marks along the bearing. In rough compass work, in the green light segment, you should have been able to check a bearing on the compass while running. But in the yellow light phase, you need to stop to let the needle come to an absolute rest for a positive bearing.

Pace Counting If the spaces between the check-off points in a yellow light segment become tricky, with too many or too few details, it may be necessary for you to measure distances on the map and to pace count these distances in the field.

With a little practice, you will soon be able to judge long distances in the field. If your map has the magnetic north-south lines preprinted or you have drawn them on your map yourself at 1-inch intervals, you know that the distance from a feature on one line on the 1:24,000 map to a feature at a right angle to it on the next line is 2,000 feet in the field. Half the distance between two lines would be 1,000 feet; one-quarter of the distance, 500 feet; and so on. If your map is a 1:12,000 map, the distance between two lines would be 1,000 feet in the field. Your thumb may actually be 1 inch wide, and the distance it would cover would be 2,000 or 1,000 feet, respectively.

For shorter distances and for more exact measurements, you will need to use the inch or millimeter ruler that is engraved on the front edge or on the side of your orienteering compass.

But whether you measure by one method or the other, you still have to translate the number of feet arrived at into steps or, better, into paces; that is, double-steps, which you count each time you put your left foot (or right foot) to the ground.

You have probably already determined the length of your pace in walking on level ground, as described below. For advanced orienteering, you will need to know the length of your pace over various terrains and at different slopes.

If the distance between two check-off points is 400 feet and the length of your walking pace is 5 feet, you know that 80 paces of walking will cover the distance. But the minute you run uphill or downhill, the length of your pace will change and the number of steps it takes will be different.

If you have tested your pace, you will know the difference. If you haven't, the following table will give you an idea of the number of paces needed to cover certain terrains by the general kind of "jog-running" commonly used in orienteering.

Terrain	Number of paces for 100 feet	Number of paces for 100 meters
Level road or path	15	50
Grasslands or meadow	17	56
Open forest	20	66
Dense forest	25	83
Uphill (depending on slope)	30+	100+
Downhill (depending on slope)	−10	−35

In other words, you can expect to be taking twice as many paces going uphill as you will on a level road, but one-third fewer going downhill.

When you become a skilled orienteer, you will learn to take your measurements in terms of paces instead of feet. If you are mathematically minded, you can do this by measuring map distances by inches or centimeters, translating them into feet or meters, and dividing the result by the length of your pace. Or you may do what a lot of smart orienteers do: develop a pace scale for running on level ground, which you glue to the front of the base plate of your compass and thus save yourself a lot of figuring. Such pace scales for map scales 1:10,000, 1:15,000, and 1:20,000 would look like this if made for a person with a pace length of 42 to 43 paces for 330 feet (1,000 meters):

These scales give the number of paces to take for a measured distance on the map under average terrain conditions. Adjustments will have to be made for rougher or more easily traveled routes, or you can have an additional pace scale, for very rough terrain or for very easily run trails or open terrain, glued to the other side of the compass plate. (The basic idea has been developed and copyrighted in Norway by Willy Lorentzen. This does not prohibit you from making your own pace scale.)

Precision Orienteering (Red Light)

The part of your route from the attack point to the control is the most critical of your journey. The imaginary signal light is definitely flashing red. Your success in reaching the control now depends on the way you practice precision orienteering, with full attention to precision map reading, precision compass setting and following, and precision measuring and pace counting.

Precision Map Reading As you approach the control, it becomes imperative for you to know exactly where you are for every pace you move ahead. This will require that you match even more check-off points in the field with their symbols on your map and make even more intensive use of the map reading by thumb method.

To do this reading correctly, you have to slow down. The seconds spent in precision map reading will be amply repaid by the accuracy with which you can now move toward the control. For the final distance to the control, it may be necessary, or certainly safest, to depend entirely on the compass, especially if the control is located on a small terrain feature.

Precision Compass Setting and Following Precision costs time—but even elite orienteers are willing to pay the time it costs to take the last critical compass bearings and follow them exactly.

To set the compass for complete accuracy, you will most certainly want to follow the example of the experts and come to a complete halt for the moment it will take you to hold the compass firmly on the map and twist the housing to the precise bearing.

Similarly, to follow the compass with precision, you will also halt completely for the few seconds it takes for the compass needle to come to rest.

Precision Measuring and Pace Counting One final thing is required. Before you continue toward the control, measure the exact distance to it and quickly translate the measurement into paces. By doing so, you will know the spot where the control should be, so that you will not, by chance, overshoot the mark.

With precise knowledge of the map features, precise setting of your compass, and precise number of paces determined, you can proceed with confidence and speed directly to the control.

And there it is: the terrain point with the orange and white marker you have worked so hard to reach! Quickly check the code number of the marker to be sure that it matches the code number on your description sheet. It does. Clip or punch your card with the punch at the control, orient your map, and reset your compass for the next leg. And off you go, until the finish banner tells you that you have completed the race.

The Postmortem

As soon as you are checked in, mingle with the other competitors who have completed the same course as you and take part in a friendly postmortem discussion. You'll have a great time sharing tales with others. You'll have a chance to compare route choices, as everyone chats about the advantages and disadvantages of the routes they decided on.

Such discussions will introduce you to new people, but they will also be of great value to you in future orienteering efforts. You will have a chance to evaluate each route selection from different points of view, and you'll pick up valuable hints, information, and pointers that might otherwise have escaped your attention.

Organizing an Orienteering Event

The requirements for organizing and running an orienteering event depend on the scope of it. A simple event can be handled by a couple of interested people, while a large event will require complex organization with a dozen or more officials with clearly defined duties.

Don't get discouraged. Quite frequently, enthusiasts who have learned orienteering elsewhere take the initiative to introduce the sport near home with a small event. It is possible for one person to take care of most of the details for a small-scale effort, from map preparation to course planning and setting to handling start and finish arrangements. You may decide to organize an easy orienteering event for your family and neighbors or for a local Scout troop or other youth group. You can run it with a few friends. It will work out!

Generally speaking, in a small club, a few enthusiastic orienteers can arrange a race for club members in a few days. For a larger event, far more planning and groundwork are necessary. Large international events and the World Orienteering Championships take years of preparation. You can imagine the organization needed for the five-day O-ringen orienteering race held every year in Sweden. With over 24,000 racers and others involved and almost two hundred different classes, every detail from showers to media coverage has to be carefully orchestrated.

If you are very ambitious and wish to start with a larger effort, you might want to seek help from an orienteering club in a neighboring area. There are quite a few good publications available on how to organize an orienteering event through the United States Orienteering Federation. There is even all sorts of computer software to help run events. Large or small, sophisticated or relatively primitive, it is rewarding to take the initiative to organize orienteering meets because the participants usually really appreciate the opportunity.

Preparing the Course

If you are a member of an active orienteering club and have proven yourself a skilled orienteer, sooner or later you may be called upon to act as a course setter for an event scheduled by your club. In accepting, you will be undertaking the most challenging involvement in orienteering but also the most enjoyable part. Your job as an active orienteer was to solve problems set by someone else for finding your way from control to control. As the course setter, it will be up to you to create problems for others to solve. You need to come up with problems that are interesting, challenging, and fair. Recruit a couple of enthusiastic helpers and go to work. Other members of the club will assume the responsibility of establishing and staffing start and finish areas and of acting as registrars, recorders, timers, and other officials, so that you can focus on the course.

Selection of Territory

Your first task is to select an area for the event. To be considered suitable, the territory should contain landscape features that will require the use of all the skills of good orienteering in a degree of difficulty fitting the abilities of the participants. You must get permission to use the area and you must make sure maps are available.

Suitable Territory

The territory for an orienteering event should be well-wooded, naturally undulating nature, preferably with little or no human habitation. It should, if possible, be an area that few of the participants have ever seen, so that no advantage is given to people who are familiar with it. A state or county park, possibly surrounded by large land holdings, might be ideal.

The territory should be well supplied with readily distinguishable features, suitable for control locations and attack points. However, it should also be of such character that accidents are unlikely to occur. Avoid places with dangerous slops, old quarry pits, bogs, and the like.

The territory should have prominent, well-defined boundaries, such as a main road, a railroad track, or a river. If possible, it is good to have roads or trails by which anyone going astray or wishing to drop out can locate the finish point without too much difficulty. Such "escape lines" are particularly important in the case of beginners or very young orienteers. They will know that by traveling a "safe bearing," easily determined by compass, they can find their way back to civilization. Exceptions to these rules may be made in competitions for orienteering experts who are expected to find their way under all circumstances.

Finally, the territory should provide a suitable start area with space for parking and some arrangement for storing equipment and personal belongings. Toilet facilities should be available at the start and finish, and at larger races, showers should be considered.

Permission of Landowners

Before undertaking any extensive work, you, as course setter, should make certain that whoever owns the territory will permit its use for orienteering on the day scheduled. This also applies to public lands.

In some instances, permission may be granted on the basis of a written request. Often you will have to appeal in person, thoroughly explaining the activity and promising to follow all guidelines. In this day and age of litigation, check whether insurance is an issue. Generally, the orienteering clubs or Scout troops will have coverage. It is possible to get one-day, special-event insurance, if necessary. You may need liability waivers for private landowners. Find out what is needed, since it is better to be safe than sorry.

Map of the Territory

For competitive orienteering, it is imperative to have a good map. For the preliminary steps in course setting, a 1:24,000 U.S. Geological Survey map of the area should suffice. In the case of state or county parks, maps are usually readily available.

For the use of participants on the day of the race, it may very well be that special maps must be prepared, based on the maps available. You may have to make corrections for changes that have occurred since the maps were printed. You can add details to the standard USGS maps to make them more like official orienteering maps by adding IOF symbols, vegetation, and declination lines. The more detail, the more interesting and fun orienteering is.

As orienteering becomes more popular, it is becoming easier to find maps made for the purpose. Such maps are usually 1:15,000 or even 1:10,000, with colors, symbols, and legends specific to orienteering. Local O clubs would be your best source for finding areas with orienteering maps.

Setting the Course: Desk Work

With the territory chosen, permission granted, and map secured, you are ready to get to work . . . at your desk. Start by studying the map of the territory. If you are an expert orienteer, the symbols on the map will seem to take three-dimensional shape. The contour lines will rise into hills and mountains, the blue lines will turn into winding rivers, and so on.

Using your imagination, scan the map for the most significant and most challenging control positions the territory has to offer. Set about marking such locations in as many different variations of the landscape as possible. If you are a smart course setter, you won't mark on the map directly, but on a clear plastic overlay or a clear plastic folder. You will change your mind many times. There is software available to help draw maps and design courses, but we are presuming you're not quite that sophisticated yet!

There are no absolute rules that dictate the form and character of the course, except for events sanctioned by a national orienteering association, official championships, or formal international events. Otherwise, there are no absolute standards for the length of the course, for the distance between control points, or for the number or placements of controls. The creation of the course is left to the course designer, with consideration to the expected participants' abilities and ages. The quality of the course depends on the course setter's orienteering knowledge, imagination, and judgment, although decisions will of course also be determined by the available terrain. Nonetheless, there are certain considerations that should always be kept in mind.

General Considerations for Course Setters

Orienteering versus Running Since the expert use of map and compass is the dominant test in orienteering, the course should be set in a way that challenges the mental ability of using the skills of orienteering, rather than simply the physical ability of cross-country running. The fastest person should not necessarily be the winner.

Variety A good course will offer variety. It should afford opportunities for both map reading and running by compass, but the emphasis should be kept on using the map, with the compass as a secondary tool. If possible, it should provide racing through all sorts of terrain—through forests, along roads and paths, over fields and meadows, and over or around hills. Forests should predominate. The legs between controls should be of different lengths, the controls of varying difficulty.

Route Choice More important than anything else, the course for an orienteering event should provide the participants with the greatest challenge possible in selecting their own routes for finding their way from one control to the next. It is here that the orienteer's ingenuity, powers of concentration, and overall skill are subjected to the most severe test.

Difficulty of Course Finally, the course must be adapted to the ability and age of the participants. Expert orienteers will expect a rugged course of a demanding length with many challenging control points. Juniors and beginners will need a course that is short in length with only a few, easy-to-find control points. Generally, the following table suggests suitable course lengths and numbers of controls for different age groups, although special ability and experience may mean that a competitor should enter a more difficult course than age alone would dictate. This example does not mean you need to segregate by age, but offers these divisions for prize distribution purposes. You can offer them by just color and difficulty, but for awarding winners it is nice to have different categories for the different courses.

Class	Course	Miles	Kilometers	Number of controls and difficulty
Beginners and Wayfarers	White	1–1½	Under 3	6–10, easy to find
Girls and Boys 14 and under	Yellow	2–3	3½–4½	6–10, easy and average
Girls and Boys 15–16	Orange	2–3	4–5	8–12, average
Girls 17–18, Women over 60, Men over 65	Brown	2–3	3½–4½	8–12, difficult
Boys 17–18, Women 19–20 and 35–59, Men 50–64	Green	2–3	4–5	8–12, difficult
Women 21–34, Men 19–20 and 35–49	Red	3–4½	5–7	8–12, difficult
Men 21–34	Blue	4½–8	7–12	10–18, difficult

Control and Attack Points

The controls on a course should be located at objects that will give the participants different kinds of tests. Some of the controls may be placed at certain elevation features, others at man-made features, still others by water features. Each requires a special technique for reaching it.

The actual control points you choose will depend on the class of orienteers with whom you are dealing. For advanced orienteers, suitable control points may be subtle, such as "depression," "knoll," or "reentrant." For beginners and juniors, more appropriate points would be the more obvious, like "hilltop," "bridge," or "crossroad."

In a similar way, an expert might be able to get along with a fairly obscure attack point, whereas the less experienced orienteer will need one or more obvious landscape features for the attack.

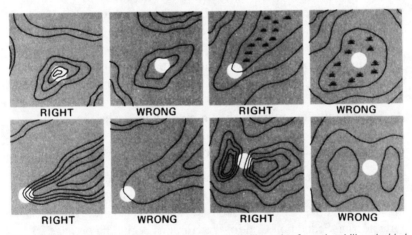

Pick suitable control points. Rights would be decided hilltop, tip of marsh or hill, or decided saddle. Wrongs would be too flat features or the middle of marsh.

The map segments on page 203, with their 6-millimeter circles, show the most commonly selected control points for orienteering. For the sake of simplicity, they are shown separated into man-made, water, and elevation features. Some descriptions:

Depression: a low point in the ground, surrounded by higher ground, shown by one or more closed contours with small "ticks"—hachures—pointing downward from the contours

Hill: an elevation, shown by two or more closed contours

Hilltop: the actual top of a hill, indicated by at least two closed contours

Knoll: a very small hill shown by a single brown dot

Pass: a passable depression between two large hills or mountains

Pond: a small body of water, less than 25 yards across

Pulpit: a projection from a hillside, shown by a contour kink

Ravine: a narrow, steep-sided valley, shown by close parallel contours

Reentrant: a minor side valley of a main valley, shown by one or more V-shaped contours

Ridge: the elongated spine of a hill, shown by one or more long, closed contours with almost parallel sidelines

Road: an unimproved dirt road, shown by parallel dashed lines

Saddle: a saddle-shaped dip between two hills or in the crest of a ridge

Spur: a minor ridge jutting out from a main ridge and generally flanked by reentrants, shown by one or more U-shaped contours

Trail: equivalent to path, shown by a single dashed line

Valley: an elongated area of low ground between two ridges, shown by wide-apart, more or less parallel contours

There are, of course, several other landscape features shown on the map that may be used as control points, such as: CHURCH, CEMETERY, MARCH, DAM, CUT, FILL, TRAIL, CROSSING, and others. See the International Orienteering Federation Control Descriptions beginning on page 233.

Before making final decisions on your control points, consider carefully the function of a control. A control is the means to the end, not the end itself. In the same way that hitting the bull's-eye of a target demands expert marksmanship, reaching a control point should demand expert orienteering skills. Finding a control should never be a matter of chance—it should mean that the orienteer has made full

COMMONLY USED CONTROLS

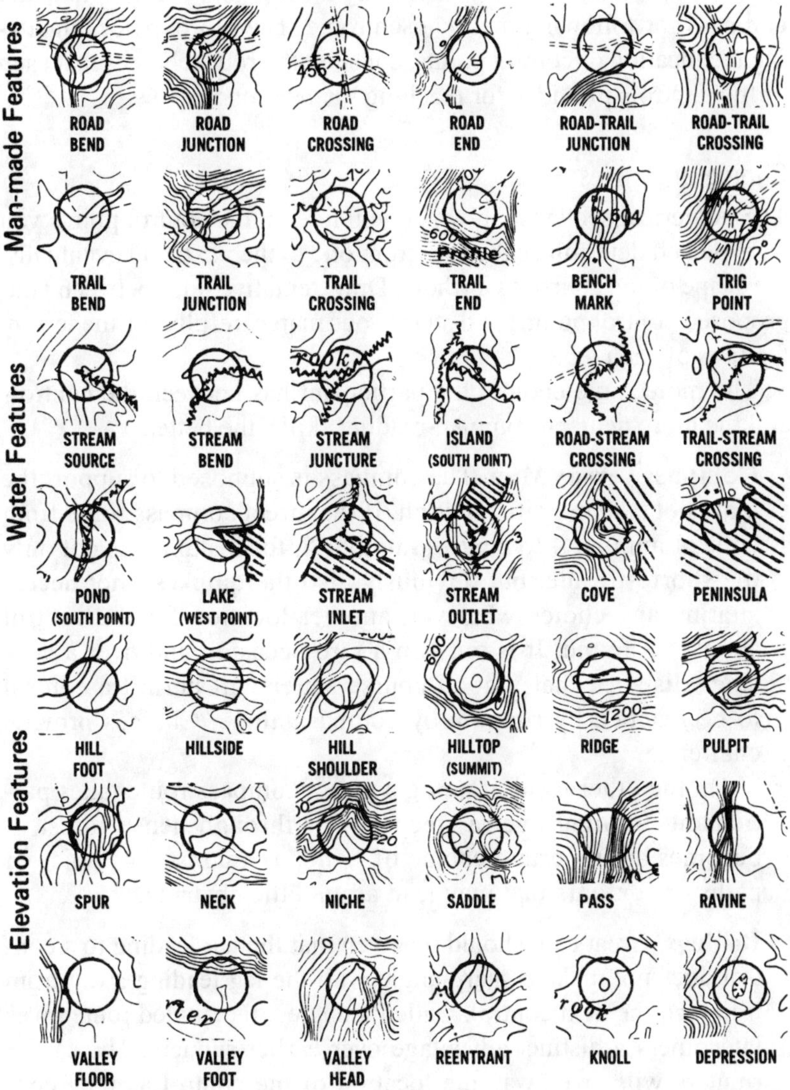

Man-made Features

| ROAD BEND | ROAD JUNCTION | ROAD CROSSING | ROAD END | ROAD-TRAIL JUNCTION | ROAD-TRAIL CROSSING |
| TRAIL BEND | TRAIL JUNCTION | TRAIL CROSSING | TRAIL END | BENCH MARK | TRIG POINT |

Water Features

| STREAM SOURCE | STREAM BEND | STREAM JUNCTURE | ISLAND (SOUTH POINT) | ROAD-STREAM CROSSING | TRAIL-STREAM CROSSING |
| POND (SOUTH POINT) | LAKE (WEST POINT) | STREAM INLET | STREAM OUTLET | COVE | PENINSULA |

Elevation Features

HILL FOOT	HILLSIDE	HILL SHOULDER	HILLTOP (SUMMIT)	RIDGE	PULPIT
SPUR	NECK	NICHE	SADDLE	PASS	RAVINE
VALLEY FLOOR	VALLEY FOOT	VALLEY HEAD	REENTRANT	KNOLL	DEPRESSION

Points used for controls may be man-made features, water features, or elevation features. Most of the above captions are self-explanatory. For descriptions of the less common features, see explanations on page 202.

use of map-reading skills in choosing a route and using a map and compass for following their chosen route. Therefore, before finalizing the location of control points, consider the route choices that each of the controls provides for reaching the next one.

Choice of Routes

The numerical sequence in which you line up the control points you have picked determines the legs from one to the next, and eventually, the shape of the course as a whole. Draw tentative lines between your proposed control points, and study your map carefully for the terrain features of each leg.

The more route choices the participant has between the controls and the more demands on map-reading skills, the better.

Compass versus Map The compass is supposed to support the map, not take over its function. If the direct compass route from control number 4 to control number 5, for instance, is not only the shortest route, but obviously also the quickest, not necessitating any choice whatever, another location for the control should be found. It is only on a rare occasion and over a very short distance that a good course setter will permit a control to be reached by running by compass alone. Choices provide challenge.

On the other hand, if going a direct compass route takes participants straight over a steep hill or through dense forest, it becomes an important choice of route, as against the choice of paths or contours that may lead around the obstacle.

Doglegs Great care should be given that the leg leading to a control does not make a sharp angle with the leg leading away from it toward the next control. Called a dogleg, the angled route gives latecomers a distinct advantage over earlier runners. The earlier runners will give away the location of the control as they continue toward the next. Of course, at larger meets that offer several courses, controls could be relatively near one another and accuracy is required to find the correct control. Following another orienteer might just lead you astray!

Handrails While the use of handrails, as explained earlier, is permissible and indeed smart for a runner, a leg that follows a handrail too closely should be avoided, except on the easiest beginner courses.

Collecting Features A large collecting feature, such as a road, a river, or a lake, invariably suggests "full speed ahead" by compass alone. To prevent such unthinking running by compass over a long distance, referred to in international orienteering as "lost kilometers," the control should never be located on the far side of and close to such a feature. It should be placed on the near side, as the runner approaches the feature, by a couple hundred feet or more. This will require the orienteer to make full use of all his or her orienteering skills, instead of depending solely on compass and running ability.

Catching Features These landmarks or terrain features lie beyond the control and can be used effectively to tell that you have gone too far. A well-designed course will have catching features suitable to the experience and skill of the participants. An orienteer who decides to use a strategy of running full speed to the catching feature and then going back to find the control will likely lose valuable time.

Hazards No route choice that a runner may decide on because it looks the shortest or the quickest should ever involve any hazardous risks, such as a falling rock area, sheer cliff crossing, or a boggy lakeshore. If it looks like some might try such a choice, pick another location for that control.

Setting the Course: Field Work

With all considerations given full attention, your course setting shifts from the desk to the field. It's time to find out if the theoretical course you set at the desk can be turned into a practical course in the field.

The most important parts of field work are to determine that the tentatively chosen control points are suitable, that the attack points are usable, and that the control and attack points are found in the field exactly where the map indicates they are located.

Checking Control and Attack Points

Nothing spoils a day for orienteers as much as a course in which even one single control has been inaccurately placed, causing them to wander about without being able to locate it, through no fault of their own. Orienteering is not a treasure hunt or a game of hide-and-seek, but a sport that calls for fair play under all conditions.

Consequently, it is necessary for you as a course setter not merely to sketch out a course on the map, but to go over the ground yourself and reconnoiter it. It is your duty to ascertain that the locations you have chosen for the controls are clearly identifiable features that are actually found where the map shows them to be. If the map does not agree with a proposed control location, the location should be abandoned. It is also your duty to make certain that attack points from which an orienteer might be expected to reach the control are correctly indicated on the map. Much of this checking needs to be done by precision compass and pace counting.

As you check each of the proposed control locations, tie a colored streamer to a nearby object. This will simplify matters when you come back to place the actual control markers just before the race.

Checking the Map

The ideal map for orienteering is one that is an exact replica of the terrain in reduced scale. The map should mirror the terrain. Such maps are, however, rare. It is difficult to produce maps that are correct in every detail, though there are professionals who provide map services, including field checking. Their work is worth the investment when you are trying to create a 1:15,000 or a 1:10,000 orienteering map.

However, from the time a map is made until you use it, things can change. New roads may have been constructed and old ones abandoned. New houses may have been built, and woods may have been cleared. Swamps may have been turned into lakes, and lakes into swamps.

Where such changes do not influence the choice of routes or the location of controls, you need to make no changes in your dispositions. But where important changes have taken place, for example, the tearing down of a bridge and its rebuilding elsewhere, updates obviously must be made on the master map and on the maps participants will use.

Finalizing the Course

The necessary field work probably cannot be accomplished on a single expedition. You may need several trips, with each exploration giving you new ideas that may change your original concept. Make the necessary alterations, finalize the control locations, and number them in the order in which they are to be visited. Then write a description list telling the nature of each control, including a code number matching the code on the marker. Each participant can then check to make certain he or she is at the right control.

As a final check, go over the whole course alone or with one of your helpers. In the latter case, have your helper do the leading, acting as a course checker. (For a major event, an official course checker, a "course vetter," is required to do the final checking.)

Maps for Orienteering

The maps needed for an orienteering event consist of a map of the area for each participant and master maps from which the participants copy onto their own maps the course they have to follow and the controls they have to visit. It has traditionally been a part of the sport to accurately copy the course. If a mistake is made there, the consequences can be tough. However, the use of master maps can be eliminated by preprinting or marking courses on the participants' maps. National and international events now require preprinting.

Participants' Maps

Each participant should be provided with a map of the course area. Many O clubs charge a small map fee as an entry fee (check when you inquire about the event). These maps can be

- a regular government topographic map of the territory (1:24,000)
- a similar topographic map published by the state or county

- a reproduction of such maps, possibly somewhat improved
- a special orienteering map, such as those required at national and international events by the International Orienteering Federation (1:10,000 or 1:15,000)

Best, as mentioned, are the special color orienteering maps, because they provide such great detail. But if they aren't available, you'll have to use what you can. If finances permit, provide each participant with a government topographic map. Or you may color-copy just the area you need, since there is no copyright on USGS maps. Modern color copiers, especially professional models, do a very good job, but check your copy carefully, to make sure all details are clear. Add more detail to it, such as the International Orienteering Federation control description symbols and colors, found on their Web site, www.orienteering .org. If you are using only a portion of the map, add necessary margin information, such as the name of the territory, the name of the event, the scale in fraction, contour intervals, and other pertinent details. Add any special instructions, such as "not all paths shown," or "not all buildings indicated." Provide the map with magnetic north-south lines 1 inch apart. Have as many copies made as you'll need for participants, volunteers, and others involved in the event.

Special Orienteering Maps

It may take a great deal of experience before you or your club decide to take on the project of making special orienteering maps, but you may eventually get there. As mentioned, such maps make orienteering even more exciting and fun. They further increase the importance of good navigation skills and fast decision-making.

Orienteering maps have been developed under the guidance of the IOF, so that they are standardized around the world. They are much more precise and detailed than regular topographic maps and are produced in larger scale (1:10,000 to 1:15,000).

Orienteering maps are developed from base maps with precise contour lines drawn from aerial and satellite photographs by modern technology. The base map will also show some major features such as lakes, creeks, roads, highways, and some trails and buildings. Many orienteering maps today are made using computer software, including one called OCAD. The completion of the map then requires substantial field work to find and locate on the map every terrain feature: small knolls, depressions, large boulders, paths and trails, ditches, fence lines, and so on.

Orienteering maps are used for championship events and national and international events. More and more O clubs are having them made for area parks. For up-to-date information on the availability of such maps, check with the appropriate orienteering federation.

Master Maps

For producing the necessary master maps, first turn your own map into a master map. To accomplish this, use a computer, or do it the old-fashioned way, with a red ballpoint pen, a template with cutouts for circles (available at art shops), and a ruler. Either way, accuracy is key!

You want to circle each control with a red circle, 6 mm (6 millimeters, or 0.6 centimeters) in diameter, in such a way that the exact—but unmarked—center of the circle is the exact location of the control. Draw a small circle to show the location of the master maps, the actual start of the event. Draw two concentric circles, 5 mm and 7 mm, to indicate the finish. For a cross-country orienteering event, number the control points in the order in which they are to be visited and connect them numerically with straight red lines. For score orienteering, mark the map with the score value of each control.

Make as many copies of the master map as you think will be needed, based upon the number of participants you are expecting. If there are, say, a hundred racers, you will want several copies of the master map so that participants don't delay one another fighting over the maps.

Control Markers for Orienteering

There is one more exceedingly important and demanding job to be done before your work as course setter is done. On the morning of the event, or if possible the day before, place the control markers in position.

Official orienteering kits, including official control markers, compasses, and control cards, can be purchased, but for beginner or informal events, you can make most of the items on your own (courtesy of A and E Orienteering).

Control Markers

The internationally recognized control marker for orienteering events consists of three squares, 12 inches by 12 inches (30 cm by 30 cm), divided diagonally bottom left to top right into two triangles. The top left-hand triangle is white, and the bottom right-hand triangle is orange-red, joined together to form a hollow prism. Each control is identified by a code, two black letters or numbers (never less than 31). The code is put on the white left-hand side, 2½ by 4 inches high (6 to 10 cm), line width ¼ by ⅜ inches (0.6 to 1 cm).

The control marker is suspended from cords in the upper corners, which can then be suspended from branches or other objects. If you are just starting out and putting on a small, one-time event for your troop or a group of friends, you can make a variation from poster board just for the day. For an informal orienteering event where money might be short, you can actually turn gallon bleach bottles or gallon plastic milk containers into control markers by painting them the standard colors. Be sure to mark each one with a separate code number, as well.

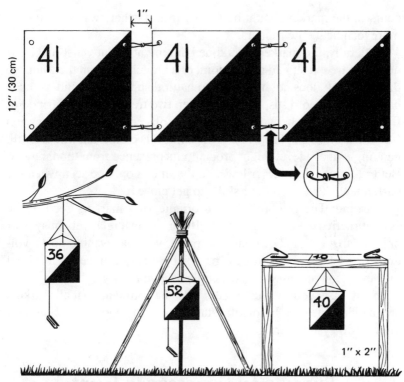

Control markers may be made by wiring together three 12-inch squares. They may be hung in trees, on tripods, or from a crosspiece between uprights.

When you get more serious, you can order official durable, weatherproof nylon controls from several sources online, listed on the U.S. Orienteering Federation Web site (www.us.orienteering.org).

Using a piece of strong cord, attach a punch to each control. Special "pin punches" can be purchased that leave a distinct mark on the control card. Electronic control e-cards are now used at bigger races, but for your unofficial races, you can use ink stampers or have people write down a specific word to prove they have visited that marker.

Placing the Control Markers

Each control marker must be put up in the exact location shown on the master map. It must be right there when the participants arrive, and clearly visible from all directions as they get near. For lower-level courses, the marker should be visible from farther away than for the more technical elite runners.

Generally, the marker should be hanging at about waist height. If hung in a tree, it should be at a point of a branch far from the trunk, so that the trunk does not hide it. If no natural support is found, you can hang it from a cord suspended between two trees, or from a tripod or from a crosspiece between two uprights placed on the exact location (see illustration on page 211). If the control is on the summit of a hill, hanging it at eye level might proclaim its presence from too far away. Better to place the marker lower so that it can only be seen when the participants have used their skills to get close by.

Warning: The brightly colored orienteering markers seem to be very attractive to souvenir hunters. If you are in a relatively busy park or other area traveled by nonparticipants, you may want to post a volunteer as guard. Explaining to passersby what orienteering is about may even convince some new people to give it a try.

In any case, you as course setter must be confident that all markers are in place one hour before the start, so that the competition director knows "all systems are go."

Running an Orienteering Event

While the course setter has been busy setting the course and preparing master maps and description sheets, in a larger, well-coordinated event, other officials from the organizing group or orienteering club have been busy as well. There will have been preliminary preparations such as sending out invitations, making and distributing fliers, and updating the Web page. Someone has been acknowledging and numbering entries if advanced entries are being taken (some meets require preregistration, others allow walk-ups). Someone may have been arranging for prizes, donations of water, portapotties, and other details. Water is crucial for drinking and for cooling down on hot days.

The day of the race, people are busy setting up the registration table at the assembly area, setting up and manning the "calling up" area, and preparing the start and finish areas.

It may seem to you that it "takes a village" to host an orienteering event from all the titles you'll read about. For larger meets, yes, you will need a lot of people to keep things running smoothly. But for a small, informal meet, a small group can wear many hats and still have a very successful event—but make sure all the jobs are assigned to someone.

Preliminary Arrangements

Before every prestigious orienteering event, invitations to participate are mailed out, though in this day and age more and more communication is by e-mail or through a Web site. If you are running your first event, be sure to contact groups or individuals you think would enjoy the day you have planned. If you are going to be open to the general public, most newspapers have free community announcement sections. Maybe you could even invite a reporter to come see what all this is about.

The invitations, fliers, and press releases should be sure to include:

1. Nature of the event (cross-country orienteering, score, relay, etc.)
2. Date and time of the event
3. Directions to the competition center and map information
4. Class divisions and course lengths
5. Date the entries should be received by the organizers
6. Entry fee and waiver forms, if any
7. Contact information for the organizing club or committee, such as an e-mail address or a phone number.

Signing Up Participants

As soon as preregistered entries start coming in, the secretary of the organizing club will write out a control card for each person, with name, club or team, start number, and class. While you can purchase special orienteering meet software, it is easy enough to create a simple system on your computer to keep track of entries—or you can even use index cards, initially.

One week before the event, he or she may e-mail or mail final information out to all preregistrants, informing them of the exact assembly point, starting time, and whatever other information may be necessary regarding parking, clothing, special conditions, and so on. The information is also posted on the club Web site. You may want to have a weather policy in place, including a rain date. Serious orienteers don't mind rain, but you want to avoid having people out in a lightning storm.

If you are allowing "day of" registration, be sure to have all materials on hand that you will need.

Day of Orienteering Event

Assembly Area

As soon as participants have arrived in the assembly area, having parked in the designated area, and if necessary changed into their orienteering outfits, they need to sign in with the registrar at the registration table. Make this table easy to find and welcoming! Names are checked off as they sign in or added if they are signing up that day. Everyone is given his or her control card, which will be needed throughout the race and which will give the starting times. The recorder will start filling in all the information on a recording sheet, though even at smaller meets this can also easily be done on a laptop computer. Everything is computer-generated at the big meets.

Participants will usually have time to mingle and talk to one another about the race and other interests. There will usually be some type of bulletin board the organizers have put up with first aid arrangements, emergency telephone numbers, the time today's event will finish, and safety rules. It may also announce future events and any member news and provide a complete list of all of the day's participants.

Start Area

Orienteering events generally have a set way of organizing participants so that everyone starts smoothly at the correct time. Be polite and friendly as you herd people through the procedure that has been set.

RECORDING SHEET								
EVENT _____ PLACE _____ DATE _____								
NAME	No.	Team	Class	Start Time	Finish Time	Time Used	Controls Missed	Position

The recording sheet may be developed as shown above. It records all the pertinent information relating to each participant. A computer can make this an easy job.

Calling Up Customarily, participants are called to the starting area by an official caller about five minutes before their start time. Someone is assigned to collect the control card stubs, if there are any, and someone makes sure the participant gets a map and a description list of the control points, if the map is not premarked. If it is premarked, they will have to wait until the actual start (no peeking!).

The Start The customary way to start an orienteering race is to move the participant up to the starting line to be sent off by a blast from the starter's whistle or horn. The timekeeper calls out the departure time from a stopwatch, while the time recorder enters it on the recorder's sheet. Electronic timers are used at many bigger meets.

Another way, as described on pages 173–175, is to start participants off in three-minute intervals.

Three Minutes before Start: Participant is "called up to the line," entering the back "get in" row of the starting grid.

Two Minutes before Start: At the starter's whistle, the participant advances to the next square in the grid, the "get ready" row. If the map is not premarked, the orienteers will generally be looking at their description lists and the map.

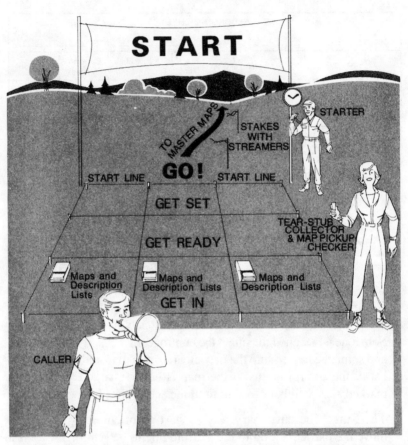

The start area requires only a few officials to send off the orienteers. The most important function is the recording of starting times.

One Minute before Start: At another whistle blast, the participant moves into the front row, the "get set" row. When the marks are premarked with the location of controls used, they would be distributed here, but no one may look at them until the "zero-minute," or start whistle. (Note: The description sheet is necessary even if the maps are premarked, because the competitors still need to know the location and other control features.)

Zero-Minute: At a third blast from the starter ("Go"), the participant takes off. The timekeeper or recorder records the departure time or checks it off against the prepared starting list.

Master Map Area

If premarked maps are used, the participants are off and running. If, however, you are using master maps as described in the earlier section for orienteers, you, as race organizer, will have to arrange a special master map area. In this case, the first part of the course will consist of a short trail of 100 to 300 feet, marked with different color streamers. White, yellow, and red (blue for elite) are traditionally used to identify the different levels of courses. The appropriate color leads to that course's master map. The trails should be set out so that the master map area is out of sight of the start.

Each participant follows the trail at full speed to the master map that has the course on it for his or her particular class. The master maps, as developed by the course setter, are mounted on pieces of plywood or other hard material. To prevent damage from weather or fingerprints, they should be covered in plastic sheeting. The participant very carefully copies the control points and the course outline onto his or her own map.

As soon as this is done, the participant takes off from the master map area, marked on the map with a small triangle, toward the first control, marked on the map with a small circle. He or she will also have the course description card, which in words or international symbols gives a clue as to where the control is. It is good to start using the internationally standard symbols (see the International Orienteering Federation Control Descriptions beginning on page 233), but for beginners, words such as "near a bend in the trail" are fine. In fact, for true beginners a clue card with increasingly detailed hints can be used.

Once the master map area is set up, it does not need to be manned, if you are short on helpers. However, official meets will have people there to guard against any cheating or confusion.

On the Course

Once participants have left the master map area, or the start area if maps were premarked, they are completely on their own. They follow the course using their best orienteering skills to find the controls in the order prescribed and their running ability to try to finish in the shortest amount of time. At each control, they punch or stamp their control card in the proper space as proof of having visited it. If, as organizer, you choose to have volunteers stationed at controls, whether to prevent theft as mentioned above or as a safety and encouragement for very young or inexperienced racers, be sure they know to be discreet. They should find a quiet place to observe and not give the control away from afar.

Finish Area

The finish area is usually located near the start area. Your helpers can be used in both positions as necessary. You will have assigned someone to set up the finish line. Sometimes a trail is set from the final control point, marked by colored streamers. The last few hundred feet

The finish area will require half a dozen or more officials. The number will depend on the number of orienteers taking part in the event.

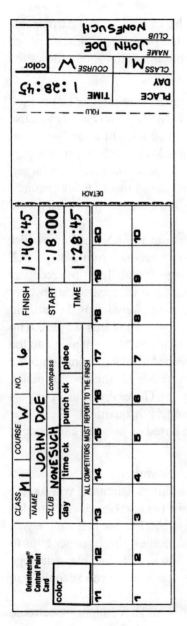

CONTROL CARD

CLASS: Men's #1. COURSE: White. TIME: in hours, minutes, seconds. NO.: Starting number.

TOP PART of CONTROL CARD turned over to control-card-stub collector at START.

BOTTOM PART of CONTROL CARD carried by orienteer and punched at controls. Turned over to control-card collector at FINISH.

FINISH according to finish-line time recorder's watch. TIME used in minutes and seconds. Transferred to top.

are best if laid through open terrain such as a field, so that participants can sprint to the finish in style. This also permits the timekeeper to see the participants as they approach the finish lines and allows the spectators to cheer everyone on.

Score Taking Finally, each participant crosses the finish line, clearly marked with a banner with FINISH on it (even if you use a bedsheet for your first race!). Again, at a small event, your volunteer helpers can have multiple jobs. Work with how many participants you expect and how many helpers you have. At a larger, official race, you will need more people to meet all the required jobs, and you will probably be going high-tech with modern timers and computers in action.

But at our smaller event, as each orienteer finishes, the time caller calls out his or her time to the nearest second from a stopwatch synchronized with that of the starting official. The time recorder writes down the time as the participant turns the control card over to the control card collector. That person carefully keeps the cards in the proper order, according to arrival times. The cards are picked up by the results runner, who brings them ten to fifteen at a time to the competition secretary's desk. The recorder puts the time onto the recording sheet and makes a note whether all the control punch marks are correct and in the right order. Generally, if any controls are missed or skipped, the participant is disqualified. The scorer (time calculator) works out the score based on minutes and seconds elapsed.

Results Board As soon as the score is worked out, it is posted on a results board by the results judge or his assistants. If you start to run races often, you may want to build a results board with wooden slats, as shown in the illustration on page 221. Another simple way is to attach cards with old-fashioned clothes pins or paper clips to a string between two trees or posts. You want to be able to arrange and rearrange people's names as they come in so you keep them in the right, winning order.

Of course, a big international race would have a fancy electronic scoreboard, but I bet we've had just as much fun.

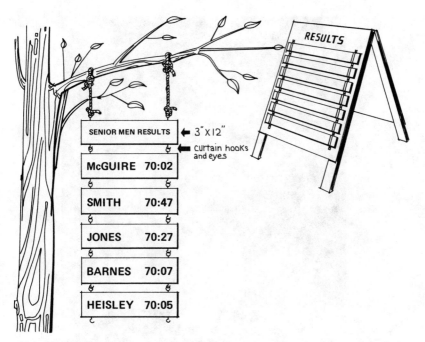

The result board may consist of wooden slats hung together or placed on a sheet of plywood.

Presentation of Prizes It is nice to have a short awards ceremony as soon as the race is over. Most people like to hang around a little while to exchange tales of their course choices and the funny or unexpected things that happened. People also like awards! The competition organizer and his or her helpers may have had trophies and ribbons made for the different levels of racers or may have solicited awards from the community (gift certificates from sports stores, restaurants, etc.). It is always nice to have small competitor's ribbons for all the younger runners, win or lose, and for those trying it for the first time.

Conclusion

Map and compass skills are useful in so many ways. Following the directions and trying all of the exercises in this book should have led

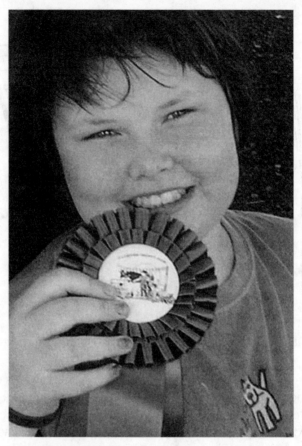

It is always great to win a prize for your efforts.

you to a point where you feel comfortable doing what you want to do in the great outdoors. Whether it is for feeling confident on a hike in a local park or while wilderness hunting and trekking, experience and practice are key. Maybe you have now tried orienteering, whether for map and compass skill practice or as a competitive sport. You may even have decided to help pass these skills onto others. Whatever your ambitions and achievements, we hope you continue to enjoy and help protect nature's many treasures.

Answers to Tests

Map Symbol Quiz (page 34)
1. Road (improved dirt)
2. Contour lines (hill)
3. Cemeteries
4. Railroad (single track)
5. Spring
6. Well
7. Buildings
8. Benchmark
9. Marsh
10. Trail
11. Bridge (river, road)
12. Triangulation station
13. River (streams)
14. Road (unimproved dirt)
15. Sand dunes
16. Church
17. School

Contour Quiz (page 37)
1. (a) almost level
2. (a) from bottom of map to top of map
3. (b) a slow grade
4. (a) a slow-moving stream

5. (a) Hutton Hill
    (c) Niger Marsh
    (e) Huckleberry Mountain

Contour Matching (pages 37–39)
A: 6   B: 1   C: 4   D: 3   E: 2   F: 5

Direction Quiz (pages 45–46)
1. 358°   2. 97°   3. 252°   4. 80°   5. 106°

Distance Quiz (page 48)
1. 7,100 feet
2. 2,900 feet
3. 21,400 feet
4. 4,000
5. 12,200

(Distances are figured from the center of one landmark to the center of the other. Permissible error: 100 feet more or less.)

Finding Places on the Map (pages 50–51)
1. Glenburnie
2. Crossroads (455)
3. Crossroads (432)
4. Church (cemetery)
5. Crossroads (432)
6. Hill 384
7. Road-T (441)
8. Road-Bend
9. Crossroads (455)
10. Start of stream

Schoolyard Compass Game (pages 89–91)
1. AEOUZP
2. EIULPA
3. IOLZAE
4. OUZPEI
5. ULPAIO

6. LZAEOU
7. ZPEIUL
8. PAIOLZ
9. AIUZAE
10. EOLPEI

Compass Competition (pages 94–96)

Start Point 1: Destination Point 7
Start Point 2: Destination Point 19
Start Point 3: Destination Point 2
Start Point 4: Destination Point 8
Start Point 5: Destination Point 16
Start Point 6: Destination Point 8
Start Point 7: Destination Point 8
Start Point 8: Destination Point 9
Start Point 9: Destination Point 15
Start Point 10: Destination Point 19

Compass Setting Quiz (pages 117–118)

1. 94°   2. 4°   3. 292°   4. 262°   5. 224°

(Bearings are figured from the center of one landmark to the center of the other. Permissible error: 2 degrees more or less.)

What Do You Find? (pages 118–118)

1. Church
2. Road-T, Glenburnie
3. Top of Record Hill
4. Road-T (381)
5. Marsh

Glossary

aiming off   a method by which the orienteer aims to one side of a control instead of directly at it.

attack point   an easy-to-find feature shown on the map from which the final approach—"attack"—to the control may be made.

back-reading   looking back over the compass toward the point from which you came.

base plate   the rectangular plate of the orienteering compass on which the compass housing is mounted.

bearing   originally the nautical term for the direction of an object from the ship. In orienteering defined as "a direction stated in compass degrees."

cardinal points   the four principal points of the compass: north, east, south, and west.

catching feature   a feature beyond the control that can be used to alert you that you have gone too far.

check-off features   features along your route that help you confirm your position on the map.

checkpoint   a conspicuous feature in the landscape shown on the map and used by the orienteer to check progress.

clue card   *see* **control description**. Some organizers will provide a clue card, especially for beginner orienteers, that is more detailed than the regular control description.

collecting feature   an obvious feature between you and the control that helps guide you.

compass   instrument for determining directions with the help of a strip of magnetized steel swinging on a pivot.

compass, conventional a compass generally enclosed in a watchcase-type of housing.

compass, orienteering *see* **orienteering compass**.

contour interval the distance in height between one contour line and the one next to it.

contour line an imaginary line in the field along which every point is at the same height above sea level.

contouring a method of traveling around an obstacle, such as a hill, by keeping at the same elevation, thus following a contour.

control one of several locations in the field to be visited by the orienteer during an orienteering event. Marked on the master map by a red circle, and in the field by a prism-shaped orange-and-white marker.

control card a card carried by the orienteer, to be marked at designated controls in a prescribed sequence.

control description a sheet or card with a brief explanation of the nature of the controls to be visited, with code numbers coinciding with the numbers on the control markers. Visit www.orienteering.org for symbols used in international orienteering events.

control punch usually a pin punch, placed at a control, to be used in punching the control card as proof that the orienteer has visited the location. At some events, electronic punching systems are used.

cultural features man-made landscape features: roads, buildings, etc.

declination the angle between the direction the compass needle points and the true-north line; the difference in degrees between magnetic-north direction and true-north direction in any given locality.

description sheet *see* **control description**.

dial, compass the rim or edge of the compass housing, usually marked with the initials of the cardinal points and graduated in the 360 degrees of a circle.

direction the relative location of one landscape feature to another. *See also* **bearing**.

direction-of-travel arrow the arrow on the base plate of the orienteering compass that points in the direction of travel when the compass is oriented.

handrails a longish feature shown on the map running more or less parallel to the direction to be followed.

housing   the part of the compass that houses the needle; on orienteering compasses, liquid-filled and turnable.

hydrographic features   water features: streams, lakes, etc.; from Greek *hydro*, water, and *graphein*, to write.

hypsographic features   elevations: hills and valleys; from Greek *hypso*, height, and *graphein*, to write.

index pointer   a line on the base plate of the orienteering compass against which the degree number of the dial on the compass housing is read.

intercardinal points   the four points of the compass between the four cardinal points: north-east, south-east, south-west, north-west.

International Orienteering Federation (IOF)   the organization governing international orienteering competitions, www.orienteering.org

landmark   a feature in the landscape that can be readily recognized— anything from a prominent tree or rock, to a church or a lake.

latitude   distance in degrees north and south from the equator.

leg   a stretch of country to be negotiated between controls.

longitude   distance in degrees east and west from the meridian through Greenwich, England.

magnetic lines   lines on an orienteering map pointing to magnetic north.

map   a reduced representation of a portion of the surface of Earth.

map symbols   small designs used on a map to indicate the features of a landscape.

master map   a map on which the controls of an orienteering event are marked and from which each orienteer marks his or her own map at the start.

meridians   lines on the map or imaginary lines in the field running true north to true south.

orientation   the process of determining one's location in the field with the help of landscape features, map, or compass, or with all three combined.

orienteer   a person who orienteers, that is, who participates in the sport of orienteering.

orienteering   the skill or the process of finding your way in the field with map and compass combined.

orienteering compass   a compass especially designed to simplify the process of finding your way with map and compass. Usually has its compass housing mounted on a rectangular base plate in such a way that it can be turned easily.

orienting arrow arrow marking or parallel lines in or on housing of orienteering compass; used for setting the compass.

orienting, compass holding a compass in such a way that the directions of its dial coincide with the same directions in the field.

orienting lines of compass the lines on the inside bottom of the compass housing parallel to the N-S orienting arrow of the compass housing; also called "magnetic-north lines" or "compass meridian lines."

orienting, map turning a map in such a way that what is north on the map corresponds with north in the field. Done by "inspection," or with the help of a compass.

pace double-step.

pace counting measuring distance by counting the number of double-steps taken.

pace scale a special scale giving the number of paces to take for a measured distance on the map, selected for the individual and based on his or her step length.

protractor instrument used for measuring angles, usually in degrees.

quadrangle a rectangular tract of land depicted on a map.

route the way taken between two controls.

scale the ratio between a distance on the map and the actual distance in the field.

steering mark an easily identifiable feature in the landscape not shown on the map, used by the orienteer to follow a bearing.

topographic maps maps with contour lines and of high precision; from the Greek *topos*, place, and *graphein*, to write.

variation another term for declination.

wayfaring a leisurely form of orienteering in which enjoyment of nature takes precedence over the competitive aspects of the sport. Commonly called map hiking.

Map and Compass Resources

General Information
Our Web site, www.beexpertwithmapandcompass.com, provides updated links and other information related to this book.

Maps
U.S. Geological Survey
U.S. Department of the Interior
12201 Sunrise Valley Drive
Reston, VA 20192
Telephone: 1-888-ASK-USGS (275-8747)
Web site: www.usgs.gov
The source for topographical maps of the United States.

Natural Resources Canada
Web site: www.maps.nran.gc.ca
Topographical maps for all of Canada.

Orienteering Organizations
International Orienteering Federation (IOF)
Web site: www.orienteering.org
Find international orienteering news, regulations, links to country federations, international control symbols, and more.

U.S. Orienteering Federation
P.O. Box 1444
Forest Park, GA 30298-1444
Telephone: 404-363-2110
Web site: www.us.orienteering.org
Excellent resource for finding local clubs, meets, orienteering maps, and other resources.

Canadian Orienteering Federation
Web site: www.orineteering.ca
The Canadian site for all things orienteering.

Equipment Sources
Several brands of good quality orienteering compasses based on the original Silva system are available today, including Silva, Nexus, Brunton, and Suunto. Larger retail sporting goods stores and Web sites carry these reputable brands. For compasses and other specialty orienteering supplies, check listings at www.beexpertwithapandcompass.com and www.us.orienteering.org.

Fun Tip
Web site: www.scouting.org
The Boy Scouts of America offer a merit badge in orienteering as well as a useful merit badge handbook.

International Orienteering Federation Control Descriptions

The International Orienteering Federation (IOF) standardized the symbols used on control description sheets to eliminate language barriers among racers and organizers and to encourage international competition. For local meets and beginner orienteers, it is fine to give no clues or to write clues out in words, but it can be fun to add to the challenge by introducing this international element. Remember, these were created for use with a true orienteering map, where details such as boulders, wells, and the like are identifiable.

The international control sheets now follow a set format that provides a lot of information, including control number, feature, appearance, and location of the control flag. The symbols are logical and fairly easy to understand. You can find most of the symbols beginning on page 237; they are also available on the IOF Web site, www.orienteering.org. Even if you are just starting your orienteering career, it is a great idea to start using and learning the symbols right from the beginning. Simple practices for memorizing the symbols can be made by copying only the symbols and having people try to identify them, or by placing symbols on index cards and matching. As a group leader, you can also create complete imaginary course sheets and have your charges working on reading them.

At the bottom left of page 234 is a sample control description sheet from the IOF International Specification for Control Descriptions. When printed, the sheet boxes should be square, with a side dimension

---

Control symbols courtesy of the International Orienteering Federation.

of between 5 and 7 millimeters. At first glance it may in fact leave you feeling lost! But in very little time you will be orienteering through the description sheet as easily as you hope to be finding your way through the woods with your map and compass. The box to the right shows how an experienced orienteer would read this sheet.

The control description is designed to be a symbolic way to give greater precision to the orienteer in his map reading and ultimate quest for the course control markers. People from all countries are on equal footing, since no language is used.

Looking at the sample, you can easily identify the name of the meet in the first row (in this case, IOF Event Example).

The second row shows the class or division numbers so that you are sure to be on the right course! For smaller meets, they could be described as the "yellow course," or "juniors' course," for example. In this case, a large international meet, we are studying the course description for the men's 45-years-and-up class (M45), the men's 50-years-and-up-class (M50), and the women's 21-years-and-up class (W21).

The third row is the course code. The first column shows the course number, because at a large international meet the different divisions will run several courses over several days. This is course number 5 for the age groups specified above. The next column indicates the length

IOF Event Example							
M45, M50, W21							
5				7.6 km		210 m	
▷				/	/	Y	
1	101						<
2	212	↖	▲		1.0		O‧
3	135	✳	✳				⊡
4	246	|†|	⊖				⊙
5	164	→	⬚				‧O
O‑ ‑ ‑ ‑ 120 m ‑ ‑ ‑ →							
6	185	/	↰				⌐
7	178	⊳					ʰO
8	147	⇌	⊓⊓		2.0		
9	149	/	/	X			
O‑ ‑ ‑ ‑ 250 m ‑ ‑ ‑ →O							

Control Descriptions for IOF Event Example		
Classes M45, M50, W21		
Course number 5	Length 7.6 km	Height climb 210 m
Start		Road, wall junction
1	101	Narrow marsh bend
2	212	North western boulder, 1 m high, east side
3	135	Between thickets
4	246	Middle depression, east part
5	164	Eastern ruin, west side
Follow taped route 120 m away from control		
6	185	Stone wall, ruined, south east corner (outside)
7	178	Spur, north west foot
8	147	Upper cliff, 2 m high
9	149	Path crossing
Follow taped route 250 m from last control to finish		

of the course in kilometers to the nearest 0.1 kilometer (7.6 km), and the third column is the amount of "height climb," or vertical climb, the course presents to the nearest 5 meters, which in this case is 210 meters. Both measurements are very important to know so you are prepared for what you are getting yourself into!

The fourth row gives the start location. The example indicates that the start will be at the junction of a road and a wall.

Starting with the fifth row, we are going to learn to read the columns for the description of the individual controls.

The illustration below shows the column letters and what they are used for. If we analyze the second control in our example, we can read in column A that this is the second control. Remember, you must visit them in the order given unless you are competing in a Score Orienteering course.

Column B is the control code, which may interest you if the number is given on the control so you can verify that you are at the right marker, and so organizers have a way to verify that the control punch you came back with is the one they assigned to that control (in this case, number 212). The IOF requires these codes be a number greater than 30.

Column C is for identifying the feature being used, if there are similar features in the area. In our example, we learn there is more than one control feature (in this case a boulder) in the area and that the one you are seeking is the north-western one.

Column D is the control feature you are looking for to help focus your map reading and find the proper control. It would be the feature at the center of the circle that defines the control site. Here we are told it is a boulder, since the dark triangular symbol is the one the IOF has chosen for this feature.

A	B	C	D	E	F	G	H

A B C D E F G H

| 2 | 212 | ＼ | ▲ | | 1.0 | O- | |

A	Control number
B	Control code
C	Which of any similar feature
D	Control feature
E	Appearance
F	Dimensions / Combinations
G	Location of the control flag
H	Other information

Column E is blank in our example, but is there in case the course setter needs to tell the competitors more information about the appearance of the control feature that is not indicated on the map. It might be particularly low, deep, overgrown, or marshy. This column may also be used when two symbols are necessary (see control 3 in our example, where the control lies between two thickets).

Column F is for the description of dimensions or combinations. It might be the height or depth of the feature in meters. It is usually given when what is shown on the map is not to scale. In our control 2 example, we learn that our boulder control feature is one meter tall—useful information when trying to decide if your map and compass skills have gotten you to the proper boulder. If the crossing or junction symbol is given here, it means that the features in columns D and E either cross or meet here. It might be a path crossing or a road junction.

Column G tells the location of the control flag or marker with respect to the control feature. No symbol is required if the control marker is positioned at the center, or near center, of the symbol. In our example, control number 2 is shown to be on the east side of the one-meter-tall north-western boulder!

Column H is for other information useful to the competitor including the location of refreshments, first aid, and a manned control.

There may also be instances where special instructions are given. They should be in the body of the description sheet and are used to reemphasize something on the map or tell you if a marked route is to be used away from a certain control or between controls. In our example on page 234, there is a special instruction given between control markers 5 and 6. It says that you are to follow a taped route 120 meters away from control 5. Why? There is no way to know from the example, but it could have to do with some safety concern. Perhaps there is a giant bee's nest, a new sink hole, or quick sand in another direction that is not on the map or might be overlooked. It might have to do with not interfering in some other activity. At any rate, you must follow the directions as given.

The last row of the example on page 234 shows the distance from the last control to the finish and whether it is taped or not. Our example shows that you should follow a 250-meter-long taped route from the last control to the finish. A taped run at the end of the course allows for a big sprint to the finish and to glory!

IOF International Control Description Symbols

This list represents most of the symbols used by the IOF. For a full listing, visit the IOF Web site, www.orienteering.org.

Column C: Which feature, if there are similar ones nearby

↑	Northern
↘	South eastern
⊟	Upper
⊟	Lower
⏛	Middle

Column D: The Control Feature

LAND FORMS

	Terrace
	Spur
	Re-entrant
	Earth bank
	Quarry
	Earth wall
	Erosion gully
	Small erosion gully
	Hill
•	Knoll
	Saddle
	Depression
	Small depression
V	Pit
	Broken ground
✳	Ant hill

Column D *(continued)*

ROCKS AND BOULDERS

	Cliff, rock face
	Rock pillar
	Cave
▲	Boulder
	Boulder field
	Boulder cluster
	Stony ground
	Bare rock
	Narrow passage

WATER AND MARSH

	Lake
	Pond
	Waterhole
	River, stream
	Minor water channel
	Narrow marsh
	Marsh
	Firm ground in marsh
	Well
	Spring
	Water tank, trough

VEGETATION

	Open land
	Semi-open land

Column D *(continued)*

	Forest corner
	Clearing
	Thicket
	Linear thicket
	Vegetation boundary
	Copse
	Distinctive tree
⊗	Tree stump/root stock

MAN-MADE FEATURES

	Road
	Track/path
	Ride
	Bridge
	Power line
	Power line pylon
	Tunnel
	Stone wall
	Fence
	Crossing point
■	Building
	Paved area
	Ruin
	Pipeline
T	Tower
	Shooting platform

Column D *(continued)*

- ⊙ Boundary stone, cairn
- ↑ Fodder rack
- △ Charcoal burning ground
- ⧋ Monument or statue
- ⊓ Building pass through
- ⌐ Stairway

SPECIAL FEATURES

- ✕ Special item
- ◯ Special item

Column E: Details of Appearance

- ⌒ Low
- ⌣ Shallow
- ⋃ Deep
- ▦ Overgrown
- ⋮⋮ Open
- ▲▲ Rocky, stony
- ≡ Marshy

Column E *(continued)*

- ▒ Sandy
- ♠ Needle leaved
- ♣ Broad leaved
- ⌐\ Ruined

Column F: Dimensions of the Feature

DIMENSIONS

- 2.5 Height or depth
- 8 x 4 Size
- 0.5 / 3.0 Height on slope
- 2.0 / 3.0 Height of two features

COMBINATIONS

- ✕ Crossing
- ⅄ Junction

Column G: Location of the Control Flag or Marker

- ⊙ North east side
- ⊙ South east edge

Column G *(continued)*

- ⊙ West part
- ⟩ East corner (inside)
- ⋁ South corner (outside)
- ↙ South west tip
- ⟨ Bend
- ⟍ North west end
- ‖ Upper part
- ⸽ Lower part
- ⋂ Top
- ⌐·⌐ Beneath
- ⌊ Foot (no direction)
- ◯ᴸ North east foot
- ⊡ Between

Column H: Other information

- ✚ First aid post
- ⛉ Refreshment point
- ⚡ Radio or TV control
- 🚶 Control check

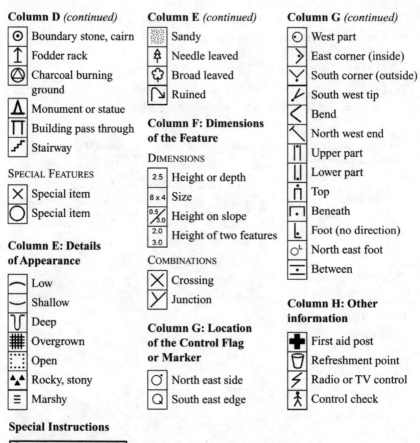

Special Instructions

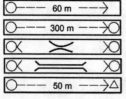

◯─── 60 m ───→	Follow taped route, 60m away from control.
◯─── 300 m ───→◯	Follow taped route, 300m between controls.
◁ ✕ ◯	Mandatory crossing point or points
◁ ⟺ ◯	Mandatory passage through out of bounds area
◯─── 50 m ───→△	Follow taped route, 50m to map exchange.

Route from Last Control to Finish

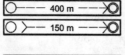

◯─── 400 m ───→◉	400m from last control to finish. Follow taped route.
◯⟩── 150 m ───→◉	150m from last control to finish. Navigate to finish tunnel, then follow tapes.
◁ ✕ 380 m ◉	380m from last control to finish. Navigate to finish. No tapes.

Index